Chinese Qigong
ILLUSTRATED

Yu Gongbao

NEW WORLD PRESS

First Edition 1995

ISBN 7 – 80005 – 247 – 8

Published by
NEW WORLD PRESS
24 Baiwanzhuang Road, Beijing 100037, China

Distributed by
CHINA INTERNATIONAL BOOK TRADING CORPORATION
35 Chegongzhuang Xilu, Beijing 100044, China
P. O. Box 399, Beijing, China

Printed in the People's Republic of China

Contents

INTRODUCTION

The length and quality of man's life is a subject of enduring importance to society. The study of the balance between health and sickness has produced numerous sparks of wisdom and constitutes an important part of the scientific and cultural heritage of mankind. The history of mankind is essentially an account of man's constant efforts to understand and perfect himself, as well as trying to understand and adapt to nature, and simultaneously attempting to change nature. These efforts have resulted in the continuing progress of society and the development of the human body, freeing both the society and the body from various constraints and bringing them closer to ultimate freedom. As a by-product of these efforts, *qigong* (breathing exercises) has been passed down from generation to generation, forming part of mankind's great cultural heritage.

Since the dawn of time, man has been aware of the necessity to train and protect himself. A good physique is a prerequisite for a healthy life, and without this man would not be able to withstand extremes of temperature. This awareness led to the appearance of *qigong* in China.

As Lü Buwei, a prime minister during the Qin Dynasty (221-207 B.C.), stated in his *Lü Shi Chun Qiu* (Master Lü's Spring and Autumn Annals), "when *yin* (the dark side) is inert and *yang* (the light side) is obstructed, the human body's *qi* (vital energy) remains unable to flow and the bones and muscles become contracted, thus they need strengthening and relaxing through dance. This has been the case since ancient times." These simple dances were created before the Shang Dynasty (16th-11th centuries B.C.) and are used to relax joints, to help the *qi* circulate freely and to nourish the internal organs. They were an early form of the use of *daoyin* (physical and breathing exercises) to aid recuperation from illness. People added mental exercises to their physical activities, in order to give expression to their feelings. The structure and style of *qigong* has intimate links with the introspective observation that is typical of Chinese culture. For example *qigong* takes harmony as its guiding principle, classical Chinese philosophy as its theoretical base, the use of willpower as its fundamental means, a combination of *dong* (motion) and *jing* (stillness) as its form of expression and physical and mental work as its goal.

Qigong has had various forms, and its name and emphasis may have varied according to the form. However, its oldest and most diverse form is *daoyin*, which holds an important position in the traditional Chinese art of preserving one's health. *Dao* refers to the fact that physical movements are guided by the strength of the mind and in turn stimulate the internal flow of *qi* within the body. *Yin* means that with the aid of physical movements, *qi* can reach the bodily extremities (for example the fingers, feet and head). In this way the flow of *qi* links the *zang* (solid organs) and *fu* (hollow organs), before returning to its starting point. The basic methods of *daoyin* are *kai* (opening) (Diag 1), *he* (closing) (Diag 2), *xuan* (rotating) (Diag 3), *rou* (rubbing) (Diag 4), *tui* (pushing) (Diag 5), *an* (pressing) (Diag 6) and *fen* (separating) (Diag 7). There are many postures and movements in *daoyin* exercises, but the emphasis is on achieving a state of harmony between body and mind. This can be done with the help of the movements, not solely because of the movements themselves, and when you reach a certain level in practice, you can even forget what you are doing, and this is "gaining the true essence of *qigong* and forgetting physical movements." This state of harmony culminates in the practice of *jinggong* (static exercises).

Daoyin has many differences from gymnastics and other modern sports, as *daoyin* exercises are based on mental activity and therefore it is possible to accumulate and conserve one's energy whilst practicing *daoyin* exercises. However, the practice of modern sports requires showing off one's strength and skill, and therefore the consumption of energy.

Daoyin developed into a fairly systematic art for the preservation of health in the Warring States Period (476-221 B. C.). For example, a book compiled during this period, *Huang Di Nei Jing* (The Yellow Emperor's Internal Classic), contains records of *qigong*, many of which deal with methods of practice, symptoms, effects and points for attention. In the book a dialogue between Huang Di and a renowned doctor stresses the combination of medical treatment with *daoyin* exercises. "Regulating the flow of blood and *qi*, taking medicine whilst observing *yin* and *yang* and calming the mind by relaxing the bones and muscles." This may be regarded as a brief summary of the principles and effects of the *daoyin* exercises.

Daoyin gained more development during the Han Dynasty (206

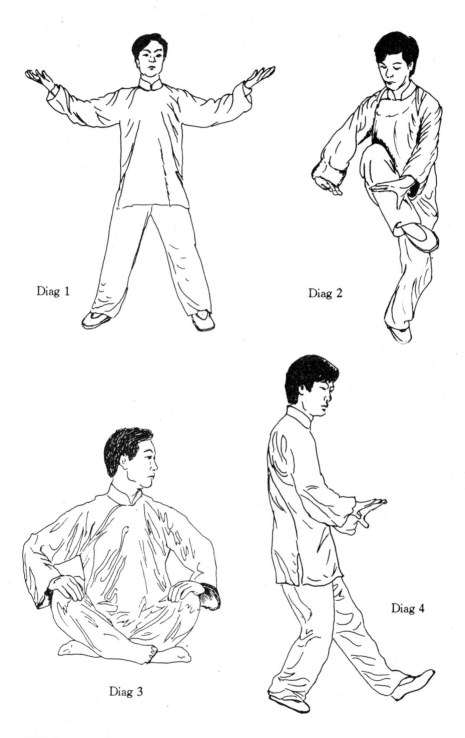

Diag 1

Diag 2

Diag 3

Diag 4

Diag 5

Diag 6

Diag 7

INTRODUCTION

B.C.-220 A.D.), when it received widespread recognition. A painting was unearthed from a tomb of the Western Han Dynasty at Mawangdui near Changsha, capital of Hunan Province in 1973. This picture vividly depicts *daoyin* movements and the effects they would produce upon certain diseases. This also demonstrates that people living at that time had already attained a certain level of fitness through *qigong*.

Another form of *qigong* exercises is *tuna* (exhaling and inhaling), otherwise known as *tiaoxi* (regulating breath) or *shiqi* (absorbing *qi*). This is a synthesis of different breathing skills. As is common knowledge, man lives on natural *qi* or air and mental activity is closely associated with the regulation of breathing. The basic train of thinking for *tuna* is that as far as possible one should expel the stale and stagnated air and inhale fresh air, thus improving the functioning of the internal organs.

There are several discussions on *tuna* in the early records of *qigong*. The most systematic are those given by well-known philosophers Lao Zi, who was living in the Spring and Autumn Period (770-476 B.C.) and Zhuang Zi (369-286 B.C.). In the sixth chapter of *Dao (Tao) De Jing* (Classic of the Way of Power), Lao Zi said, "The spirit of the valley is immortal and mysterious femininity. The gateways of mysterious femininity (the nose and the mouth) represent the sources of heaven and earth. One should exhale and inhale in a soft and continuous manner as if breathing itself does not even exist." In the 29th chapter of the same book, he gives a vivid description of how to expel stale air and inhale fresh air, saying, "You can advance or retract, and breathe gently or forcefully." Zhuang Zi also gives an explanation of *qigong* in his book, placing a high value on the role of *tuna* in prolonging life. Furthermore an essay unearthed together with a *daoyin* diagram from a Han Dynasty tomb at Mawangdui may be regarded as a classic treatise on keeping fit using *tuna*. This essay *Que Gu Shi Qi* (Taking Less Food and Absorbing *Qi*) is over 400 Chinese characters long and written on a long piece of silk. It explains how and when to absorb *qi*, how frequently to do it a day and other special points for attention, so it is of great value for people today. Moreover, a few special articles and books on *tuna* have appeared since ancient times, most of which have been written by Taoist masters.

There are a number of *tuna* skills which can be divided into three basic categories.

1. *Koubi huxi* (breathing through the mouth or nose). In the practice of *qigong* the most common method of breathing is to inhale

gently through the nose but exhale slowly through the mouth. Inhaling and exhaling through the nose is also important, but can only be used when a higher state of *jing* (stillness) is reached. The third method is to inhale and exhale through the mouth, but this is seldom used.

2. *Fushi huxi* (abdominal breathing). The method, which has both normal and abnormal usages, is practiced by focusing attention on contracting and extending the abdomen, whilst inhaling and exhaling. The normal method of *fushi huxi* requires you to keep the abdomen relaxed and extended whilst inhaling but contracted whilst exhaling, whilst the abnormal method of *fushi huxi* means that you keep your abdomen contracted whilst inhaling and relaxed whilst exhaling.

3. Other methods of breathing and regulation. These are usually used in conjunction with mental activity and include such methods as *chongqi* (filling the body with *qi*), *dantian huxi* (directing *qi* to *dantian*, a region two or three centimeters below the navel), *zhongxi* (directing *qi* to the heel), and *guixi* (breathing like a tortoise).

There are two further types of *tuna* exercise, one of which is performed with the aid of physical movements. When this is done, breathing must be connected with the movements in order to improve the overall effects. Thus the internal and external exchange of *qi* should be maximized and the flow of *qi* around the body smooth. (Diag 8) However, these movements must be performed in the correct manner. In general, the movements for inhalation are "close," (Diag 9) whilst those accompanying exhalation are "open." (Diag 10)

In the early stages of the development of *qigong*, *tuna* had its own exercises, but as the exercises increased in number and the principles that these were based upon were perfected, *tuna* exercises became incorporated into those of other schools of *qigong*. This reflects the general trend of *qigong* development.

The third form of *qigong* exercises is *neidanshu* (the training of active substances in the body), which became the main stream of *qigong* over a long period of time. (Diag 11) *Neidanshu* appeared in the Han Dynasty and began to take shape in the Tang Dynasty (618-907). During the Song (960-1279) and Yuan (1279-1368) dynasties it was further developed and therefore it shall receive more attention than any other forms of *qigong* exercise.

The roots of *neidanshu* are in *waidanshu* (the production of immortality pills). In ancient times some magicians believed that medicine following a certain prescription might help prolong life. This aroused great interest among some emperors such as Emperor Qin Shi Huang

Diag 8

Diag 9

Diag 10

Diag 11

(259-210 B.C.) of the Qin Dynasty, Emperor Wu Di (156-87 B.C.) of the Han Dynasty and Emperor Tai Zong (599-649) of the Tang Dynasty, who all sent messengers to look for or make "immortality pills." Their desire for immortality pills encouraged the development of *waidanshu*. In fact, the so-called immortality pills were made of gold, stone and other chemical substances (for example mercuric sulfur, copper and arsenic). Because of their toxicity they caused many deaths. It was for this reason that people turned their attention to *neidanshu*, a form of exercise which would improve the functioning of internal organs. Wei Boyang of the Eastern Han Dynasty (25-220) wrote a book on the above-mentioned two methods, but he emphasized the *neidanshu* principles and exercises. In time *waidanshu* proved useless to the art of health preservation, but it did contribute to chemistry, metallurgy and other forms of science and technology that emerged in ancient times.

Neidanshu is a form of exercise which helps one to keep healthy that transforms *jing* (the essence of life) into *qi*, *qi* into *shen* (mental activity) and *shen* into *xu* (nothingness). When performing this exercise *dantian* can be regarded as a stove, *shen* can be seen as fire and *jing*, *qi* and *shen* as medicine. *Guanqiao* (the special regions of the human body) is of great importance in these exercises. Most of these regions like *dantian*, *mingmen* (located on the back), *shanzhong* (located on the chest) and *xinghai* (between the eyebrows) are acupuncture points. The development of *neidanshu* has made the system of *jingluo* (main and collateral channels) more complete and systematized its medical theories and principles. The use of the mind is also important in order to focus attention on a certain body part, and in so doing, special results can be gained. (Diag 12)

Aiding the flow of *qi* is not only a method widely used in *qigong* but also an old *neidanshu* exercise. When this exercise is performed, the internal *qi* must flow along certain channels and fork off at some special regions. An article titled *Xing Qi Yu Pei Ming* written by a *qigong* master during the Warring States Period gives a detailed description of how to aid the circulation of *qi*. The most popular *qigong* practice is *zhoutian* (creating a big or small circle of *qi*). The big *zhoutian* allows the *qi* to flow along the *jingluo* system and spread across the body, whilst the small one refers to the practice of allowing *qi* to flow up along the *Du* channel and down along the *Ren* channel. The practice of *zhoutian* exercises will familiarize one with the concept of *qi* and its effect upon the body.

Cunxiang (concentrating on a certain object or person) is a form

14   INTRODUCTION

Diag 12

of mental activity in *neidanshu*. Its function is to relax the whole body, aid both combination and exchange of substances within the body, and place mind and body in perfect harmony. *Cunxiang* consists mainly of *waiguan* (looking outside) and *neishi* (looking inside). *Waiguan* means focusing one's attention on something outside the body, like the sun, the moon, a river or a mountain, whilst *neishi* refers to concentrating the mind on a part of body, such as an internal organ. It should be mentioned that *neidanshu* is normally practiced by Taoists and therefore strongly influenced by Taoism, thus making Taoists objects of mind concentration.

There are several books on *neidanshu*, but many of them are complicated and abstruse. Their explanations of this practice differ wildly, which may account for the appearance of its various schools. When you trace their origins, it can be seen that they generally have their roots in two schools—the southern and northern. The southern school was established by Zhang Boduan during the Northern Song Dynasty (960-1127), whose book *Wu Zhen Pian* (On the Real Meaning of *Qigong*) has since been studied and annotated by *neidan* masters in later years. Zhang's book and their notes on it offer a theoretical basis for the southern school of *neidanshu*. The northern school, created by Wang Chongyang during the Jin Dynasty (1115-1234), branched out into the Longmen school with the help of his disciple Qiu Chuji, and produced far-reaching effects upon the development of *qigong*. The northern school made further contributions to the development of *qigong*, and among other things, made a systematic study of exercises for women.

Sun Buer, another disciple of Wang Chongyang's, wrote several books on the differences between men's and women's *qigong* as well as stating the principles that women should follow and the points to remember during practice. That was said to be a breakthrough in *qigong* development.

Qigong has many functions, yet the most basic of these is to improve health, so it has always been regarded as a means of treatment, especially in ancient times. Its basic doctrines, such as *wuxing* (five elements), *yunqi* (five elements' *dong* and six kinds of natural factors), *guaxiang* (eight trigrams) and *maixiang* (pulse condition) conform with the basic tenets of traditional Chinese medicine. The principles and methods to be followed in *qigong* practice has been given special space in books on traditional Chinese medicine. The whole book *Huang Di Nei Jing* has grown out of the concept of *qi* and in the book descriptions of *qigong* exercises are given. These can also be found in many other books such as *Zhu Bing Yuan Hou Lun* (A General Treatise on the Causes and Symptoms of Diseases) compiled in the Sui Dynasty (581-618), in which around 200 sets of exercises are listed for over 100 diseases. Doctors have praised the effects that *qigong* may have upon diseases.

Hua Tuo (?-208) of the Eastern Han Dynasty (25-220), who is held in high esteem in the Chinese medical world, created *wuqinxi* (five-animal play), a kind of *qigong* exercise still popular across the country today. Tao Hongjing (452-536), a specialist in the art of preserving health during the Northern and Southern Dynasties (420-581), explained his ideas on keeping healthy and devoted space to a number of important exercises in his *Yang Xing Yan Ming Lu* (Notes on the Cultivation of Moral Character and Prolonging of Life). Li Shizhen (1518-1593), a great physician of the Ming Dynasty (1368-1644), emphasized the importance of coordinating *qigong* practice and medical treatment. This caused *qigong* to become a favorite subject of many doctors in the Ming and Qing (1644-1911) dynasties, and thanks to their efforts, many exercises such as *liuzijue* (six-character formula) (Diag 13) and *baduanjin* ("brocade" exercise in eight forms) (Diag 14) were created to prevent and cure diseases. Indeed *qigong* has helped improve health and prolong life. For example, Tao Hongjing was still very energetic in his eighties and Fang Kai, who had learned *yannian jiuzhuan gong* (nine-circle exercise for achieving longevity) (Diag 15) from his master and who passed it on to his disciples, was said to have a clear voice, straight back and indefatigable legs when he was 100 years old.

Diag 13

Diag 14

Diag 15

Diag 16

To improve the quality of life, one must fight against diseases and cultivate one's moral character. The importance of the latter cannot be overemphasized in *qigong* practice. The practice of *qigong* requires one to combine the cultivation of moral character with the training of the body. In order to achieve this, *zuochan* (sitting in meditation) is most effective. (Diag 16) In *zuochan* practice, the mind and body must be completely calm and relaxed, and thus one can achieve a deeper understanding of life.

Qigong has been accepted by people in all walks of life, although those living in the imperial court in ancient times were the first to practice it. However, it was not until the Han and Tang dynasties that this art of health preservation became popular among federal rulers. For example, Cao Cao (155-220), a statesman living in the closing years of the Eastern Han Dynasty, called for many *qigong* masters to gather together and swap experience. *Qigong* was further developed in the Ming and Qing dynasties, and quite a number of *qigong* masters became prominent. The 17th son of Emperor Tai Zu in the Ming Dynasty, Zhu Quan, had a keen interest in medicine and the art of health preservation. He gathered as much material as possible and, having analyzed it, put forward some new points of view. Furthermore he compiled *Ba Duan Jin Dao Yin Fa* ("Brocade" Breathing Exercise in Eight Forms), producing a profound effect upon the development of *qigong*.

The cultivation of moral character is regarded as necessary in the practice of *qigong* and has attracted attention from many scholars. Confucius (c. 551-c. 479 B. C.) and Mencius (c. 372-289 B. C.), the very founders of Confucianism, repeatedly insisted on the necessity for *yangqi* (nourishing *qi*). Moreover Neo-Confucian philosophers in the Song and Ming dynasties stated that although there were a number of ways in which to study, the most important of these was to read for half a day and spend the other half digesting what one has read. Well-known poets like Bai Juyi (772-846) of the Tang Dynasty, Su Shi (1037-1101) and Lu You (1125-1210) of the Song Dynasty were also interested in *qigong*, and some of them even expressing this interest in their poetry.

Over the years scholars have gained deep inspiration from *qigong*. Their interest in, and practice of, *qigong* has helped this art gain importance in the cultural field, through incorporating the essence of other art forms. So when one researches *qigong*, it will become apparent that it is an essential feature of Chinese culture, through which one can learn, from a unique perspective, much about the traditional way of thinking.

Qigong attaches much importance to the relationship between man and nature. When you get to learn about this relationship, you will have a clear picture of the outlook of the ancient Chinese towards life, especially their ideas on completeness, balance, imitation and harmony between *xing* (physical movements) and *shen*.

Completeness: The universe is composed of many correlating and interrelating organisms, man is but one of them. A relationship characterized by integration and harmony exists between men, and indeed between man and the universe. So when you practice *qigong*, you must use your body as a starting point to examine the relationship between your body and nature.

Balance: The most important goal is for your life to enter a state of balance, a kind of dynamic equilibrium produced by the harmony of *yin* and *yang*. Without it, you will not be able to reach a higher level of *dong*.

Imitation: Man benefits from all other things on earth, including animals and plants, and he can imitate some of their traits of life to build up a strong constitution. "*Dao* takes nature as guideline" and *qigong* itself includes quite a few movements which imitate living things. For example there are movements imitating the appearance of plants and the movements of animals like the dragon, the tiger, the deer, the bird and the leopard. These can often be seen in *wuqinxi* and *yijinjing* (limbering-up exercise for the tendons) as well as in other popular *qigong* exercises.

Harmony between *xing* and *shen* : *Shen* is a comprehensive reflection of bodily functions. It exists solely because of the human body, and in turn affects the human body itself. In *qigong*, the cultivation of both *shen* and *xing*—the purification of body and mind—is emphasized. This can be achieved in many ways, popularly including the adjustment of posture, the regulation of breath and the coordination of mental activity. The first two are known as "*yangxing*", the last as "*yangshen*."

These last four points are said to be the basic tenets of *qigong*, and various *qigong* exercises and methods have only come into being in accordance to these principles.

The human body is a complicated organism full of mysteries. *Qigong* is very closely connected with the human body and therefore can be quite abstruse, becoming all the more mysterious when it is said to be "beyond comprehension." Nevertheless, there have always been people who devoted themselves to the study of *qigong*. In order that more people should learn and practice this art, in this book the researchers illustrate their descriptions of *qigong* with vivid diagrams and figures. *Qigong* principles, exercises and skills are explained and although the diagrams and figures in this book are selected from classic books, the language used is simple and exact. These diagrams and figures can be used for reference by those who are keen to study and practice *qigong*.

The book has four sections. The first explains *qigong* theory such as *Hetu* (River Map), *Luoshu (Luo* Plan), *bagua* (eight trigrams) and *jingluo*, and *neiyao* and *waiyao* (internal and external medicine), the regular and irregular *sanguan* (two three-step processes), and *xianglong fuhu* (subduing the dragon and taming the tiger). All these diagrams have produced a profound effect upon traditional recuperative *qigong*. Some diagrams like ten *chan* pictures distinguish themselves by their innovative composition, natural charm and innate artistic taste. The second section of the book is about *qigong* exercises. To make it easier to follow, the book contains many pictures depicting a number of exercises, which are easy to learn and effective. Some of them are for *daoyin*, others for *tuna*, and others for *yishou* (mind concentration) and *xingqi* (aiding the flow of *qi*). Many of them have been accepted by other schools of *qigong*. The last two sections of the book—*Styles and Basic Requirements for Practice*—are also indispensable.

Yu Gongbao
Beijing
March 1994

THEORY

Hetu and *Luoshu*

A legend has it that a "dragon horse" was found in the Yellow River in central China during the reign of Fuxi (c. 5000 B.C.), the first ancestor of mankind in the Chinese mythology, with a diagram on its back. That was called *Hetu*. The scheme in the map served as a model for Fuxi to draw *bagua*. Later, when Yu the Great led his people to drain off the waters of a flood around 2200 B.C., a "divine tortoise" came out of the Luohe River, carrying on its back a pattern to be known as *Luoshu* later. Though scholars differ from one another in the origin of *Hetu* and *Luoshu*, these two diagrams are nevertheless widely accepted as symbols of the beginning of Chinese civilization.

Both *Hetu* and *Luoshu* contain the basic pattern that underlies the theory of *bagua* and *wuxing*. The correlation of numbers in the map and the plan express the philosophical views of the ancient Chinese on the structure and development of the world. In both diagrams, the odd numbers (1, 3, 5, 7, 9), or *yang* in nature, find expression in light circles, whereas the even numbers (2, 4, 6, 8, 10), or *yin* in nature, take the form of dark circles. And the directions of *yang* and *yin* in these two diagrams is determined when you face south, with upwardness standing for south, downwardness for north, righthandedness for east and lefthandedness for west.

In *Hetu*, one, the number of the origin of *yang*, is placed in the north; two, the number of the origin of *yin*, in the south; six and seven are the complementary numbers of one and two respectively; three, the number of the growth of *yang*, is located in the east; four, the number of the growth of *yin*, in the west; eight and nine are the complementary numbers of three and four respectively; and finally, five and ten are at the center.

In *Luoshu*, one in the north signifies the origin of *yang*, three in the east the growth of *yang*, nine in the south the abundance of *yang*, seven in the west the decline of *yang*, two in the southwest the origin of *yin*, four in the southeast the growth of *yin*, eight in the northeast the abundance of *yin*, six in the northwest the decline of *yin*, five in the center harmony between *yang* and *yin*, heaven and earth.

Hetu and *Luoshu* show a state of affairs through numbers, explain patterns through a state of affairs and reflect nature through patterns. Both of them lay a foundation for the development of the fundamental theory of *qigong*.

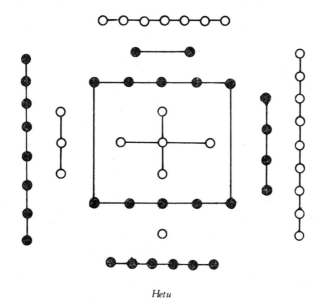

Hetu

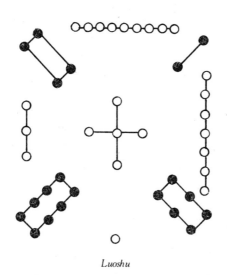

Luoshu

Taiji Diagram

The *taiji* (supreme ultimate) diagram presents an image of interaction between *yin* and *yang*. The dark area is symbolic of *yin* and the light one of *yang*, and the dark and light "fish" chasing each other stand for constant *dong* and change. The small dark and light dots in the diagram suggest that there is *yang* within *yin* and vice versa. The S-shaped dividing line, or the *taiji* line, symbolizes a state of harmony and balance. The two fish comprise a whole circle, indicating that *yin* and *yang* do coexist in the same entity and promote, check and change each other.

The human body, in health or sickness, is regulated through the *dong* of *yin* and *yang*. *Qigong* exercises are done on the basis of regulating the *dong* of *yin* and *yang* within the human body so that balance will be achieved. In the context of the human body, *yang* usually denotes the male, the upper part of the body, the back, the limbs, the six *fu* organs (gallbladder, stomach, large intestine, small intestine, bladder and the tri-*jiao*, or warmer), whilst *yin* refers to the female, the lower part of the body, the abdomen, the torso, the five *zang* organs (heart, liver, spleen, lungs and kidneys). All the vital activities are manifest in the *dong* of *yin* and *yang*.

THEORY

Bagua

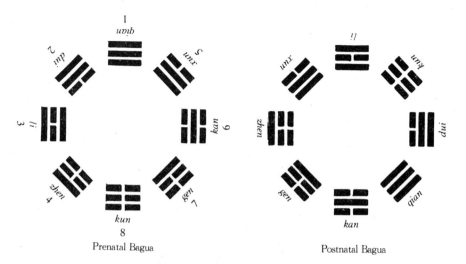

Prenatal Bagua   Postnatal Bagua

Bagua was devised by ancient Chinese, who observed the *dong* of heaven and earth and made a study of living things, including mankind, in relation to their natural surroundings. With *bagua*, these ancient Chinese depicted man and the cosmos and explained the structure and movement of the universe. In this sense, *bagua* is a map of the world.

Bagua represents the basic law of all forms of *dong* in the world — from the movement of the stars to the vital activities within the human body. Therefore, it has long served as a theoretical guideline for *qigong* practitioners.

Traditionally, there have been two versions of *bagua*. The first is the Fuxi *bagua*, or otherwise known as the prenatal *bagua*. The second is the Wenwang * *bagua*, or sometimes called the postnatal *bagua*. In the prenatal *bagua*, *qian* (heaven) is in the south, *kun* (earth) in the north, *li* (sun) in the east, *kan* (moon) in the west, *gen* (mountain) in the northwest, *dui* (river) in the southeast, *zhen* (thunder) in the northeast and *xun* (wind) in the southwest. The four trigrams, from *qian* to *zhen*, move counterclockwise and signify the *dong* of heaven, whilst the rest, from *xun* to *kun*, move clockwise and indicate the *dong* of earth. In the postnatal *bagua*, *li*, *kan*, *zhen* and *dui* form two complementary pairs, taking up their positions in the south, north, east and west, but the other four are placed at the four corners.

* Wenwang refers to Wen Wang, leader of the Zhou royal house in the closing years of the Shang Dynasty.

Spatial Outlay of *Bagua*

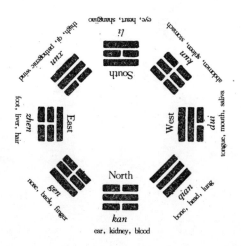

Bagua has various correlations with respect to both the natural environment and the human body.

In terms of spatial outlay, *li* is located in the south, *kan* in the north, *zhen* in the east and *dui* in the west. This design provides a guideline for many *qigong* exercises that lay emphasis on the importance of facing in the right direction during practice.

Bagua also corresponds to various parts of the human body. The interrelation between the structure and function of human organs can be shown in the correlation of *bagua*. Based on the theory of *bagua*, the *qigong* exercises that are used to regulate specific parts of the human body have been developed.

Round Diagram of the Sixty-four Hexagrams

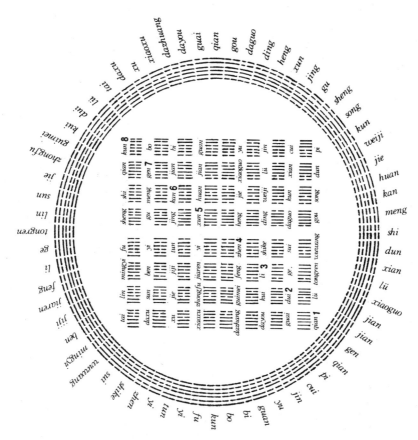

Prenatal Round Diagram of the Sixty – four Hexagrams

Bagua consists of broken (*yin*) and unbroken (*yang*) lines. Picking up two trigrams from *bagua* and placing one above the other, you will get the sixty-four hexagrams. The upper trigram is called the "outer" trigram, and the lower one the "inner" trigram.

The sixty-four hexagrams constitute the fundamental framework for the exposition of *qigong* in terms of the *yin-yang* relation. The arrangement of broken and unbroken lines in each hexagram and the correlation between different hexagrams indicate the cyclic *dong* of the human body and the natural world, which in turn provide a useful reference system for *qigong* practice.

Linear Diagram of the Sixty-four Hexagrams

The sixty-four hexagrams may be arranged in a square, circular or linear way. The linear diagram starts with *qian* and ends with *kun*, with *yin* and *yang* taking their course from *zhen* and *xun* to *kan*, *li*, *gen*, *dui*, and further to *qian* and *kun*. If divided in the middle at *hou* and *fu* into two lines, the linear diagram will become a circular one. It can also be grouped into eight hexagrams and rearranged into a square diagram with eight hexagrams on each other.

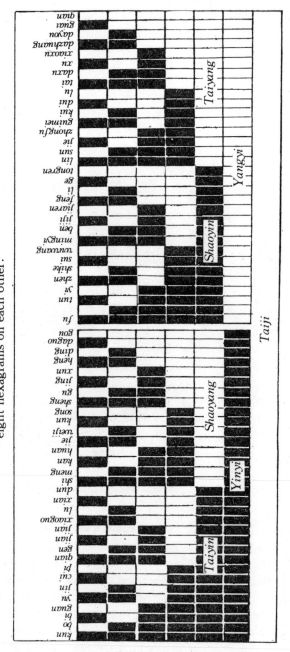

Wuxing

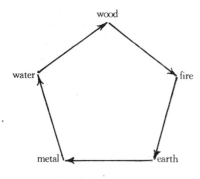

Generating and Promoting

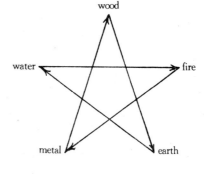

Controlling and Checking

The theory and design of *wuxing* were already widely used in medicine, health keeping, and economy and politics as early as over 2,000 years ago. The theory underlying *wuxing* deals with correspondences and correlations among various processes. Each system in the world is perceived to be in a state of dynamic equilibrium, with five processes corresponding to *wuxing* in constant interaction. *Dong* and change are shown in relation to the dynamic of the entire natural world.

Wuxing generates and promotes one another in the following sequence: fire arises from wood, earth from fire, metal from earth, water from metal and wood from water.

Wuxing controls and checks one another in the following sequence: wood is under the control of metal, metal of fire, fire of water, water of earth and earth of wood.

Wuxing and *bagua* are both based on the same philosophy. Each of *bagua* diagrams also has a corresponding phase: *qian* (☰) (metal), *dui* (☱) (metal), *li* (☲) (fire), *zhen* (☳) (wood), *xun* (☴) (wood), *kan* (☵) (water), *gen* (☶) (earth) and *kun* (☷) (earth).

Wuji

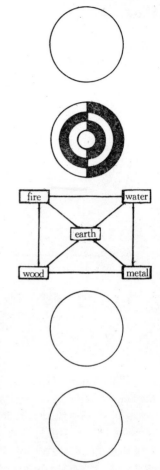

The *wuji* (supreme void) diagram dates back to the Song Dynasty (960-1279), and is ascribed to Chen Tuan, a well-known expert on the health-keeping art in that era. Later, Zhou Dunyi, a philosopher, renamed it the *taiji* diagram, reading it from top to bottom instead of from bottom to top as Chen Tuan did. The *taiji* diagram became a theoretical guidepost for *qigong* practitioners of later generations.

The diagram starts with a state of *wuji*, which in turn generates a state of *taiji* through the *yin-yang* division. The *dong* of *taiji* produces *yang*. Excessive *dong* leads to *jing* (stillness), and *jing* (stillness) results in *yin*. *Dong* comes from excessive *yin*. The interaction of *yin* and *yang* on the one hand and *jing* (stillness) and *dong* on the other is reflected in *wuxing*.

Kan (☵), with a *yang* line between two *yin* lines, represents the original *qi*. *Li* (☲), with a *yin* line between two *yang* lines, shows the genuine *jing*. *Jing* resides motionless in the body, and mental activity is regulated.

Qian represents the mind and *kun* the body. Their interaction produces all things on earth.

Clearness and Turbidness, *Dong* and *Jing* (Stillness)

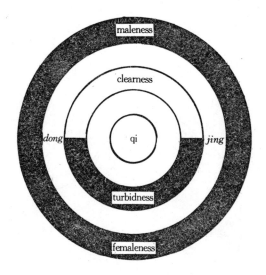

Dadao (the origin of nature) produces one *qi* (basic element), which contains both *yin* (the negative) and *yang* (the positive). *Yin* is turbid but *yang* clear, and the female is dark and the male light. Know its lightness but stick to its darkness; know its maleness but stick to its femaleness. That is the method to train both the internal organs and the limbs, and to enhance the mind and the body. Clarity is the source of turbidness and *dong* is the basis of *jing* (stillness). Remain clear and still and you will refrain yourself from taking rash action, and the *qi* in your body will return to the original state of abundance. That is one of important things for health keeping.

Nourishing the Mind

Like a sovereign ruling over his subjects, the mind controls all the organs in the body. When you are in a state of *jing* (stillness), your body will be in balance and harmony and there is little risk of coming down with diseases. Therefore, the most important is to regulate mental activity. According to *Dao De Jing*, whoever seeks the origin of nature must first look at his own mind, and the regulation of mental activity is the ultimate goal for Confucianists and Buddhists as well as Taoists.

There are two methods to nourish the mind. The first method is to look at the mind, and what you look at is called *lingtai* by Confucianists, *lingguan* by Taoists and *lingshan* by Buddhists. Direct the eyes, the ears and the tongue towards the mind. Concentrate on the mind all the time, no matter what you do. That is called *dingxing* (concentration). The second is to make the mind free of distracting thoughts. In so doing, you can find your physical movements and mental activity smooth and without obstruction.

Concentrating on *Zuqiao*

Zuqiao (a region between the heart and the navel) is also called *xuanmu*. According to *Dao De Jing*, "the gate of *xuanmu* is the root of heaven and earth." Zhang Ziyang said, "The cultivation of the golden elixir depends entirely on *xuanmu*."

Concentrating on *zuqiao* means remaining in a state of *wuji* and nourishing the original *qi*. *Dao De Jing* also states: "Too many words lead to exhaustion. It is better to concentrate attention on practice." Regulate mental activity in *zuqiao*, without too much concentration or neglect. Maintain the body like a plant supports itself with the firm roots.

Deep in concentration, the mind remains aware but does not exert itself. When the mind is still, enlightenment will come naturally; when the mind and body have forgotten each other, *shen* will assemble with the assistance of *qi*, and the force of life will combine itself with *shen*. With that the whole body will enter a state of harmony with little conscious effort.

Bringing the Three Parts Together

The meeting of the three parts means an advanced state of balance and harmony to be achieved in *qigong* practice.

The three parts refer to body, mind and consciousness. *Jing*, *qi* and *shen* are known as the three elements. Bringing the three parts together indicates the maturation of the elixir; the integration of the three elements signifies the completion of the elixir, and their meeting can be achieved through a state of blankness and *jing* (stillness). The method is: Make the mind blank so that it will combine with *shen*; keep the body still so that *jing* and emotion will be at rest. Only in that way can the three elements become *qi* with the consciousness totally untroubled.

When the body is still, *jing* will change into *qi*; when the mind is calm, *qi* will transform into *shen*; and when consciousness is at rest, *shen* will return to the prenatal state of void.

Heche

Heche (river wagon) is an exercise for the circulation of *qi* inside the body. *Jing* and *qi* move in a regular route so that the outside will be linked with the inside and the body with *shen*, with their function much like a wagon full of cargo. Hence the name *heche*.

The method to be used usually is as follows: Concentrate your attention on the exercise, and look into the body with your eyes. Then accumulate the genuine *qi* at *dantian* and direct it past the *weilu* point and up to the *jiaji*, *yuzhen* and *niwan* points before moving down to the *queqiao*, *chonglou* and *huangting* points and returning to the *dantian* region.

Heche can be big or small. With a small *heche*, you may mobilize the cyclic *dong* of *wuxing* to achieve the concentration of *qi* through the integration of water and fire. With a big one, you may generate golden elixir from behind your elbow and send it to the *niwan* point and remove lead and add mercury to produce great elixir.

Heche also refers to the original *qi* or the genuine *qi* produced in *qigong* practice. *Zhong Lu Chuan Dao Ji* (A Collection of Religious Teachings by Zhong Lu) says, "In the beginning, nourish the genuine *qi* in the kidney, which belongs to the upright water in the north. The upright *qi* produced by the original *qi* is *heche*."

Zhentu

Keep sincere, silent and gentle and have your mind in *zhentu* [*dong* (ignorance) and *jing* (stillness)]. Nourish your *qi* and make it strong and potent, without too much concentration or neglect. With *huijian* (the use of willpower) in *zhentu*, all diseases will vanish from your body.

Zhentu is the original willpower. To keep fit through *qigong*, you are required to cultivate the mind seriously. *Qi* comes from willpower, just as plants imbibe nourishment from their roots in the earth. When the soil is good, the plants will flourish. And only when you have a noble character, will you be able to make progress in *qigong* practice, and reduce or even eliminate various worldly burdens.

Take substances for medicine and you will cure your body of diseases, and take exercises for medicine and you will regulate your mental activity. To get rid of diseases and regulate mental activity, you have to look into your own mind.

THEORY

The Union of *Qian* and *Kun*

Qian is *yang* and stands for heaven. *Kun* is *yin* and represents earth. The union of *qian* and *kun* means the balance of *yin* and *yang* and water and fire in the human body.

The exercises for the union of *qian* and *kun* is also known as the big *zhoutian*. To learn this exercise, you have to keep your mind still and peaceful, shut your eyes to all around you and listen to your inside world, and concentrate your attention on the mind and breathe slowly and evenly. Thus, fire arises from water, with the midline of back like a wheel, the four limbs like rocks, the kidneys like boiling water and the bladder like burning fire. In the twinkling of an eye, *tianji* (natural law) plays its part. Then direct *qi* gently and regulate breath consciously and slowly. Let nature take its course: metal and wood blend, and water and fire rise and fall. Suddenly, something the size of a millet falls to the *huangting* point and proceeds to grow into an elixir. By then the mind and body will have become void and *shen* and *qi* are in harmony with nature.

Neiyao and Waiyao

Yao (medicine) consists of neiyao, or jing, qi and shen, and waiyao, or medicine in real life. Both kinds of yao are important in qigong practice. Neiyao is all-effective, whilst waiyao is not so all the time; neiyao has no definite shape or form but exists in the body, whilst waiyao has its shape and form but does not really exist; neiyao can promote transcendence, whilst waiyao may help treat diseases; neiyao exists in yourself, whilst waiyao comes from the human body; and neiyao clings to your body, whilst waiyao clings to the universe.

Neiyao can be produced all of a sudden but waiyao must be cultivated gradually over a long period of time. Neiyao is as important as waiyao, and you cannot do without waiyao. That is why you should cultivate neiyao whilst taking waiyao and train your mind whilst treating your body.

THEORY

Timetable for *Qigong* Practice

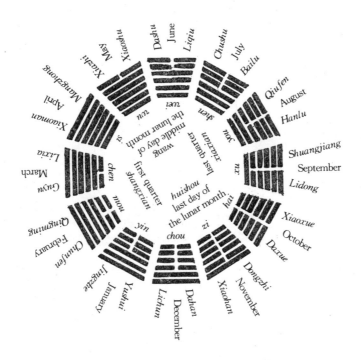

The twelve earthly branches control the 12 months, during which a cyclical change takes place in the circulation of *qi* and blood as shown in the following 12 hexagrams:

fu,   lin,   tai, zhuang, mei,   qian,

(☷) (☷) (☷) (☷) (☷) (☰)

gou,   dun,   pi,   guan,   bo,   kun.

(☰) (☰) (☷) (☷) (☷) (☷)

When you practice *qigong*, keep in step with nature and the change of the four seasons and adapt yourself to the natural conditions in each month so that you will achieve better results.

Sanguan

Sanguan (three-step process) may be regular or irregular. When you are in the regular *sanguan*, your mind will come from consciousness, your willpower from the mind, your emotion from willpower, and your wild fancy from emotion; when you are in the irregular *sanguan* your wild fancy will go back to emotion and your emotion back to willpower so that you can have willpower and mind under control and your mind return to consciousness. In other words, when you are distracted from worldly things, you are meeting with the regular *sanguan* but when your mind is free of all those things, you are having the irregular *sanguan*.

The regular and irregular *sanguan* may be explained as follows.

Dao (the mother of nature) produces *qi*, *qi* produces *yin* and *yang*, *yin* and *yang* produce elixir and elixir produces all things in the world. That is called the regular *sanguan*. Shape transforms into *jing*, *jing* into *qi*, *qi* into *shen*, and *shen* into void, and a Buddha or celestial being comes into the world. That is called the irregular *sanguan*.

The first step in the irregular *sanguan* is to transform *jing* into *qi*. To fulfill this process, make use of *yang* as soon as it appears. The second step is to transform *qi* into *shen*. In so doing, you can direct the circulation of the original *qi* in the body whilst fire is strong. The third step is to practice *shen* and then go back to void. For this goal, concentrate on the mind and *shen* will return to consciousness.

THEORY

Xianglong and Fuhu

There are various figures of speech in books on traditional *qigong*, and the dragon and the tiger are two metaphors that we often come across there.

The dragon and the tiger have different interpretations. First, they stand for water and fire each, as shown in expressions like "the dragon comes out of fire" and "the tiger grows from water." Second, the dragon refers to the original *shen* and the tiger to the original *jing*. Third, the dragon represents *shen* and the tiger stands for *qi*. They may also be used to give an idea of *jing* and *qi*, *yin* and *yang*, female and male.

Xianglong and *fuhu* are quite important in *qigong* practice. Great masters down the ages have paid great attention to getting rid of distractions through *xianglong* and to regulating mental activity through *fuhu*. *Xianglong* signifies the checking of *zhenhuo* (internal heat) in the heart, and *xianglong* will come true when the fire dies away. *Fuhu* indicates the control of *zhenshui* (liquid in the heart) in the body, and *fuhu* will be finished when the source of water becomes crystal-clear. We can also say that *xianglong* and *fuhu* are to regulate the mind, get rid of distracting thoughts and purify consciousness.

Rotation of *Falun*

With the Plough moving all the time, *falun* (wheel of exercise) rotates without a stop. *Falun* as named by Buddhists is also called *zhoutian* and *xingting* (circulation of *qi*) by Confucianists.

Yin and *yang* propel, attract and mingle with each other, and in turn cause changes in nature. Sustain *jing* and *qi* to nourish the body and cultivate *zhenji* (the moment when the prenatal and postnatal *qi* combines into one) in conformity with the law of nature and your health will improve a lot.

Method of practice: Keeping in a sitting position, start the exercise consciously but conclude it subconsciously. In the beginning, direct and rotate *qi* from the inside of the body to the outside and from small circles to large ones, with the couplet being recited silently: "The white tiger hides in the east and the black dragon lies in the *you* position on the *taiji* diagram." Rotate in a circle whilst reciting a sentence of the couplet, and you have to rotate your *qi* 36 times. When you collect *qi*, rotate it from the outside of the body to the inside and from large circles to small ones. In so doing, recite the couplet 36 times: "The black dragon lies in the *you* position on the *taiji* diagram and the white tiger hides in the east." Return *qi* to its source in the state of *taiji*. That is called one *zhoutian*. After persistent practice, no mental effort is needed to guide the movement of *qi*, and *falun* will rotate of itself.

Zhixie Tianji (Analysis of Natural Law)

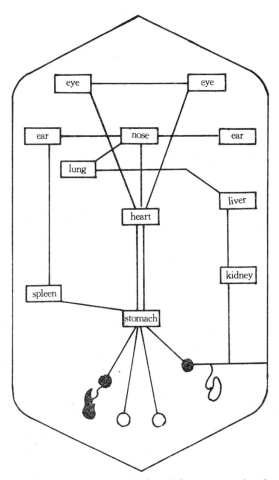

In the exercise, the eyes are inhabited by *yishen* (god of toil), the ears by *songshen* (god of send) and the nostrils by *laoshen* (god of labor).

Make the breath slow and even, close the eyes and look inside. Listen to the inside, and circulate *qi* in the body. Through this practice, *shen* returns to the tripod: the spleen *qi* and the stomach *qi* meet to connect with the heart, the liver *qi* and the gallbladder *qi* meet and go along the intestines to link with the kidneys, and the lung *qi* controls the heart *qi* and links with the nose.

Keep your mind quiet and peaceful, so that the original *qi* can circulate throughout the body, activate the internal mechanism, and *jing*, *qi* and *shen* are all strong.

Twenty-four Solar Terms

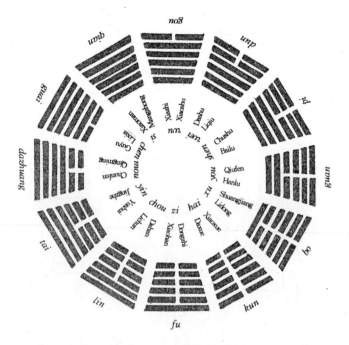

According to *qigong* theory, the natural world and vital activities undergo cyclical changes in step with the shifting balance between *yin* and *yang*. Therefore *qigong* practice should be adapted to different times of the year. Each of the twenty-four solar terms defined in the Chinese lunar calendar has a unique state of *yin-yang* balance. The dates at the beginning of each term are important times for *qigong* practice, and different exercises can be used to suit the specific *yin-yang* balance of each term.

The *yin-yang* balance of the solar terms can be represented by hexagrams. *Dongzhi* (Winter Solstice) is *fu*, with one *yang* line; *Dahan* (Great Cold) is *lin*, with two *yang* lines; *Yushui* (Rain Water) is *tai*, with three *yang* lines; *Chunfen* (Spring Equinox) is *dazhuang*, with four *yang* lines; *Guyu* (Grain Rain) is *mei*, with five *yang* lines; *Xiaoman* (Grain Full) is *qian*, with six *yang* lines; *Xiazhi* (Summer Solstice) is *hou*, with one *yin* line; *Dashu* (Great Heat) is *dun*, with two *yin* lines; *Chushu* (Limit of Heat) is *pi*, with three *yin* lines; *Qiufen* (Autumn Equinox) is *guan*, with four *yin* lines; *Shuangjiang* (Frost's Descent) is *bo*, with five *yin* lines; and *Xiaoxue* (Slight Snow) is *kun*, with six *yin* lines.

Ten *Chan* Pictures

Chan (meditation) is a state in which you gain wisdom and enlightenment through self-cultivation. There are many methods of achieving this state, including *zuochan*, *xingchan* (walking quietly) and *wuchan* (contemplation). Self-cultivation is an advanced skill in Buddhist *qigong*. Bojo Guksa, a Buddhist monk living in the Ming Dynasty (1368-1644), wrote ten poems and drew ten pictures to describe the steps to enlightenment through contemplation. The buffalo in the pictures stands for the natural character of man or the source of life.

(1) In the Wild

Troubled by all kinds of thoughts and desires, people are liable to get nervous and disturbed in daily life and with their natural character confused and the ability to sustain themselves lost, they are quite ill with various worries and diseases. The poem reads:

Displaying its horns, the buffalo bellows aloud,

Running along the mountain path into the distance.

A patch of black clouds overhangs the valley,

The buffalo tramples wheat seedlings wherever it goes.

Ten *Chan* Pictures

(2) Initial Training

When you start *qigong* practice, place your mind under control and set strict demands on yourself, as if fastening the buffalo with a rope. After persistent practice, you will become disciplined and avoid unnecessary losses. The poem reads:

Controlled by a rope through its nose,
The buffalo runs swiftly under the whip.
It is no easy thing to overcome a willful temper,
As the boy struggles hard to lead the buffalo.

THEORY

Ten *Chan* Pictures

(3) Under Control

After some practice, you will find yourself calm and stable gradually. But you cannot slacken your efforts at this moment, anyway. Be sure to forget fatigue and feel at home. The poem reads:

Under constant training the buffalo stops dashing,
Following the boy across streams and through clouds.
Not daring to loosen the rope in his hand,
The boy tends the buffalo all day in spite of his fatigue.

Ten *Chan* Pictures

(4) Turning Back

When you reach a certain stage in practice, a turn for the better will take place and the destination of your life's voyage will appear before you. In so doing, you can grow out of recklessness and act in conformity with nature. At this juncture, keep your mind steady and consolidate the original *jing* and strengthen the original *qi*. The poem reads:

A long time has passed before the buffalo turns back,
Its reckless temper has gradually grown gentle.
Not trusting the buffalo completely to itself,
The boy has not yet unfastened the rope.

Ten *Chan* Pictures

(5) Tamed

When you return to the true nature, you will enter a state of freedom; and when you combine the inside with the outside, you will not find yourself shrouded in dust any longer but see the light. Now that you have found your true character, you can do away with those strict demands. The poem reads:

Under the green poplar, by the ancient stream,
The buffalo moves in harmony with nature.
Returning at sunset over the fragrant meadow,
The buffalo follows the boy, who has dropped his rope.

THEORY

Ten *Chan* Pictures

(6) Getting Free of Hindrance

Getting free of hindrance is a state of penetration and evenness, and real control of both the body and the mind. Then try to enter a state of void through *qi* and *shen* practice and you will feel the inherent rhythm of life. The poem reads:

Sleeping contentedly under the sky,
The buffalo needs the whip nevermore.
The boy, sitting under the pine tree,
Starts to play a peaceful, happy tune.

Ten *Chan* Pictures

(7) In Control

A man's potential is boundless, and exploiting and making use of it will lay groundwork for the distillation of life. As the "buffalo" has been tamed and is free from worldly hindrance, it is time for you to enjoy the power of freedom and stroll in the realm of life. The poem reads:

Bathed in sunset, the river floats past the willow tree
Under the fragrant meadow in light mist.'
Totally at ease, the buffalo drinks when thirsty, eat when hungry,
And the boy is lying on a rock, deep in sleep.

Ten *Chan* Pictures

(8) False Reality

What is above everything is the true reality and observing various things in the world with a tranquil mind. Attaining the "union of man and heaven," an advanced state in *qigong* practice, you will be in harmony with yourself and with nature. The poem reads:

The white buffalo stays in the white clouds;
The boy is free of concern, and so is the buffalo.
Penetrated by moonlight, the white clouds grow whiter;
The moon goes its way, and the clouds drift by.

Ten *Chan* Pictures

(9) Single Light

With the buffalo and its master in perfect harmony, there is not any difference between the outside and the inside. *Shen* merges with the body and willpower with *qi*. Whenever illumination comes, you will feel at ease and full of go and vigor. The poem reads:

After the buffalo has vanished, the boy enjoys leisure;
A solitary cloud drifts across the hill.
Clapping his hands, the boy sings under the moon,
Though he has another portal to cross before reaching home.

Ten *Chan* Pictures

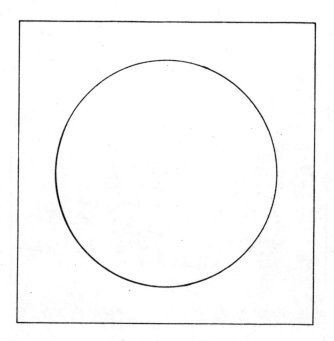

(10) Rest in Sleep

The mother of nature is formless, and everything may be back to the original purity and simplicity. The circle in the diagram shows a state of purity and perfection so that existence is non-existence and vice versa. Remaining quiet and still, you will gain ultimate wisdom and enlightenment and the purification of your life will draw to an end. The poem reads:

Both the boy and the buffalo are nowhere to be found,
The moon illuminates the vast void.
If in search of the meaning of all this,
Look at the wild flowers and fragrant grass.

THEORY

Diagrams of *Jingluo* and Acupoint

In *qigong* practice, deal with the various passages and points for the movement and accumulation of *qi*. They are known as *jingluo* and acupoints. The *jingluo* is a network of pathways linking together all the parts of the human body, whilst acupoints are sites for the exchange and confluence of *qi*. Concentrating attention on those points and massaging them can regulate the function of the *jingluo* system. The *jingluo* in the human body include the 12 regular channels and the *Ren* and *Du* channels. The 12 regular channels relate directly with the *zang* and *fu* organs.

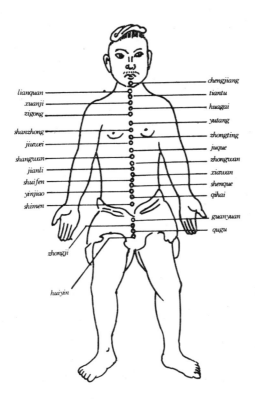

(1) The *Ren* Channel

The *Ren* channel starts below the navel and runs along the abdominal cavity to the throat and then to the lower jaw, where it goes around the lips and spreads up to the eyes in branches. It frequently crosses the three *yin* channels of the hand and foot and has the function of regulating all the *yin* channels in the body. It is therefore known as the "sea of *yin*."

Diagrams of *Jingluo* and Acupoint

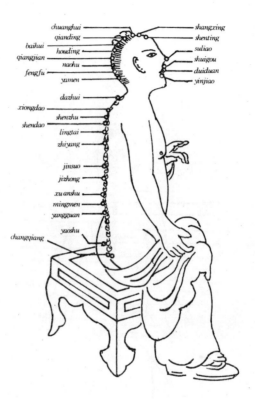

chuanghui — — shangxing
qianding — — shenting
baihui — suliao
qiangjian — houding — shuigou
naohu — duiduan
fengfu — yamen — yinjiao
dazhui
xiongdao
shendao — shenzhu
lingtai
zhiyang
jinsuo
jizhong
xuanshu
mingmen
yangguan
yaoshu
changqiang

(2) The *Du* Channel

The *Du* channel starts at the lower abdomen and runs down along the perineum. Then it turns up along the midline of the back to the *fengfu* point at the nape of the neck before going through the brain to the vertex and along the midline of the forehead to the nose. It controls all the *yang* channels of the human body and is known as the "sea of *yang*."

As two major pathways for the flow of *qi*, the *Ren* and *Du* channels have great significance in *qigong* practice, especially in the exercise called *zhoutian*.

56

Diagrams of *Jingluo* and Acupoint

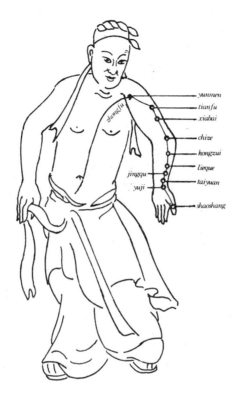

(3) The Lung Channel of Hand-*Taiyin*

This channel starts at the middle-*jiao* region where the spleens and stomach locate, and runs along the large intestine and the orifice of the stomach and through the diaphragm before entering the lungs. Then it goes transversely from the *zhongfu·* and *yumen* points along the medial side of the upper arm to the Pericardium Channel of Hand-*Jueyin*. And then it goes through the *tianfu* and *xiabai* points to the *chize* point at the elbow and runs along 'the anterior portion of the forearm by way of the *kongzui* and *lieque* points to the *jingqu* and *taiyuan* points above the main artery of the wrist. Finally it runs through the thenar eminence to the *yuji* and *shaoshang* points along the radial border and ends at the tip of the thumb.

The malfunction of the lung channel may produce cough, asthma, fullness in the chest, thirst, pain in the shoulder and back, dysphoria or sore throat.

THEORY

57

Diagrams of *Jingluo* and Acupoint

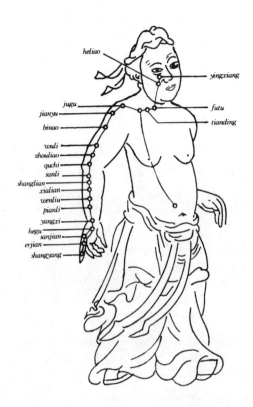

heliao
yingxiang
jugu
jianyu
binao
futu
tianding
wuli
zhouliao
quchi
sanli
shanglian
xialian
wenliu
pianli
yangxi
hegu
sanjian
erjian
shangyang

(4) The Large Intestine Channel of Hand-*Yangming*

This channel starts at the *shangyang* point at the tip of the index finger and runs up along the radial side of the index finger and the *erjian*, *sanjian* and *hegu* points to the *yangxi* point at the wrist. Then it moves first up along the lateral side of the forearm to the lateral side of the elbow along the anterior border of the upper arm to the *jianyu* point on the shoulder and back before meeting with the *Du* channel at the *dazhui* point to reach the supraclavicular fossa and the lungs, diaphragm and the large intestine. Its branch moves up along the neck, the cheek and the gum of the lower teeth to the *yingxiang* point by the side of the nose.

The malfunction of the large intestine channel may produce diarrhea, bowel sound, dysentery, toothache, dryness in the mouth and yellow discoloration of the sclera, pharyngitis, laryngitis or nasal obstruction.

THEORY

Diagrams of *Jingluo* and Acupoint

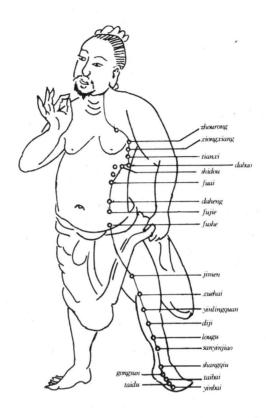

zhourong
xiongxiang
tianxi
dabao
shidou
fuai
daheng
fujie
fushe

jimen
xuehai
yinlingquan
diji
lougu
sanyinjiao
shangqiu
gongsun
taibai
taidu
yinbai

(5) The Spleen Channel of Foot-*Taiyin*

This channel starts at the tip of the big toe and runs along the medial side of the foot through the *yinbai, taidu, taibai, gongsun* and *shangqiu* points, and then along the front of the inner ankle bone, and the posterior surface of the lower leg. Then it goes up through the *sanyinjiao, lougu, diji, yinlingquan, xuehai, jimen* and *chongmen* points to the abdominal cavity. Finally it goes inside to meet with the spleen and the stomach and then runs up through the diaphragm to the root of the tongue. The malfunction of the spleen channel may produce stomachache, abdominal distention, enteritis, vomiting, edema, heaviness in the limbs and weakness, glossalgia or difficult urination.

Diagrams of *Jingluo* and Acupoint

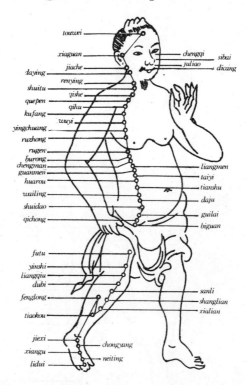

Labels (clockwise/top-down): touwei, xiaguan, jiache, daying, renying, shuitu, qishe, quepen, qihu, kufang, wuyi, yingchuang, ruzhong, rugen, burong, chengman, guanmen, huarou, wailing, shuidao, qichong, futu, yinshi, liangqiu, dubi, fenglong, tiaokou, jiexi, xiangu, lidui, chongyang, neiting, chengqi, sibai, juliao, dicang, liangmen, taiyi, tianshu, daju, guilai, biguan, sanli, shanglian, xialian

(6) The Stomach Channel of Foot-*Yangming*

This channel starts at the *yingxiang* point and runs up to the foot of the nose, down to the upper gum and around the lips before going up again to the front of the ear and further up to the *touwei* point on the forehead along the hairline. One of its branches appears at the *daying* point and runs down to the *renying* point and the supraclavicular fossa along the throat before going through the diaphragm to meet with the spleen. Another branch runs down from the supraclavicular fossa to the *qichong* point on the lateral side of the lower abdomen through the nipple and along the navel. Still another branch emerges from the lower orifice of the stomach and runs down to *qichong* and the thigh and the knee and further down to the lower leg and the instep and ends at the *lidui* point at the tip of the second toe.

The malfunction of the stomach channel may produce stomach trouble, toothache, headache, abdominal distention, bowel sound, insomnia, edema or dementia.

Diagrams of *Jingluo* and Acupoint

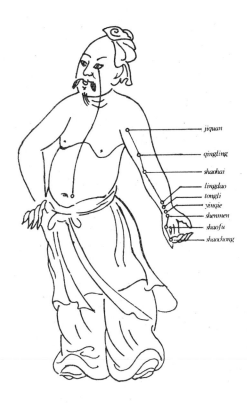

- *jiquan*
- *qingling*
- *shaohai*
- *lingdao*
- *tongli*
- *yinqie*
- *shenmen*
- *shaofu*
- *shaochong*

(7) The Heart Channel of Hand-*Shaoyin*

This channel starts at the heart and spreads in three branches. The main branch goes up to the lungs and turns down to the armpit before running through the cubital fossa of the forearm and the pisform regions to the palm along the posterior border of the medial side of the upper arm. Then it goes further down to the *shaochong* point at the tip of the little finger along its medial side and meets with the Small Intestine Channel of Hand-*Taiyang*. Still another branch goes up along the side of the throat to meet with the eye.

The malfunction of the heart channel may produce cardiac pain, palpitation, chest pain, costalgia, dry throat, thirst or insomnia.

Diagrams of *Jingluo* and Acupoint

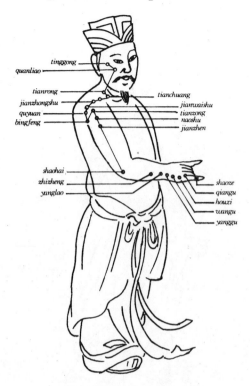

(8) The Small Intestine Channel of Hand-*Taiyang*

This channel starts at the *shaoze* point at the tip of the little finger and runs along the ulnar side of the dorsal hand through the *qiangu*, *houxi*, *wangu* and *yanglao* points, and then along the posterior aspect of the forearm through the *zhizheng* point to the *shaohai* point at the elbow. Then it moves up along the posterior border of the lateral side of the upper arm to the *jianzhen* and *naoshu* points behind the shoulder joint, and then along the scapular region through the *tianzhong, bingfeng, quyuan, jianwaishu* and *jianzhongshu* points to meet with the *Du* channel at the *dazhui* point. And then it goes up into the supraclavicular fossa and down to meet with the heart before running through the diaphragm along the esophagus to the small intestine by way of the stomach. Its branch moves up along the side of the neck to the cheek and the outer corner to the ear. The malfunction of the small intestine channel may produce sore throat, deafness, yellow discoloration of the sclera, swelling of the cheeks, pain in the shoulder and arm or distention of lower abdomen.

Diagrams of *Jingluo* and Acupoint

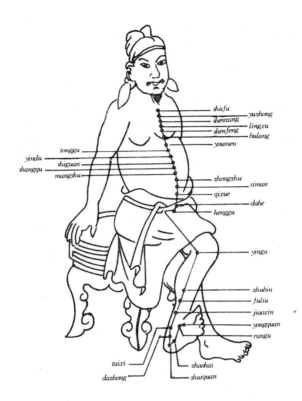

shufu
shenzang
shenfeng
youmen
yuzhong
lingxu
bulang

tonggu
yindu
shiguan
shangqu
mangshu
zhongzhu
siman
qixue
dahe
henggu

yingu

zhubin
fuliu
jiaoxin
yongquan
rangu

taixi
dazhong
zhaohai
shuiquan

(9) The Kidney Channel of Foot-*Shaoyin*

This channel starts at the inferior side of the little toe and runs up to the heel through the *yongquan* and *rangu* points along the medial malleolus before meeting with the Spleen Channel of Foot-*Taiyin* and the Liver Channel of Foot-*Jueyin* at the *sanyinjiao* region. Then it moves up to the *yingu* point at the knee crease along the medial side of the lower leg, and goes through the base of the spine along the innermost side of the thigh to meet with the kidney and the bladder. Its branch runs up from the kidney through the liver and diaphragm to the lungs and along the throat to the root of the tongue.

The malfunction of the kidney channel may produce dry mouth, chest pain, asthma, palpitation, diarrhea, poor vision or listlessness.

THEORY   63

Diagrams of *Jingluo* and Acupoint

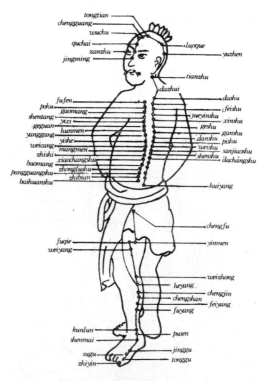

(10) The Bladder Channel of Foot-*Taiyang*

This channel starts at the *jingming* point at the inner side of the eye and runs up through the *zanzhu, quchai, wuchu, chengguang* and *tonglian* points along the forehead to the *baihui* point on the top of the head. The main channel runs through the *baihui* point to the brain and through the *luoque, yuzhen* and *tianzhu* points to the top of head before turning down along the spine to the *shenshu* point and the abdominal cavity to meet with the kidney and the bladder. One of its branches runs from *baihui* to the temple. Another branch runs down from *shenshu* to the *baihuanshu* point, where it turns up to the *shangliao* point and down again to the *huiyang* point near the coccyx before going along the buttocks and the posterior aspect of the thigh to the *weizhong* point. Still another branch runs down from the nape of the neck and through the gluteal region to a place near the *zhiyin* point at the lateral side of the tip of the little toe by way of the leg.

The malfunction of the bladder channel may produce headache, pain in the back and loin, difficult urination, hemorrhoids or enuresis.

64   THEORY

Diagrams of *Jingluo* and Acupoint

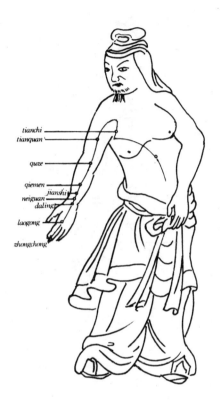

(11) The Pericadium Channel of Hand-*Jueyin*

This channel starts in the chest and the pericardium and runs down to the tri-*jiao* through the diaphragm. Its branch appears at the *tianchi* point near the armpit and runs up along the chest and the medial side of the arm and down through the *tianquan, quze, ximen, jianshi, neiguan* and *daling* points to the *laogong* point at the center of the palm and before ending at the *zhongchong* point at the tip of the middle finger.

The malfunction of the pericardium channel may produce cardiac pain, dysphoria, chest pain, oppressed feeling in the chest, dementia, swelling of the armpit, yellow discoloration of the sclera or flushed face.

Diagrams of *Jingluo* and Acupoint

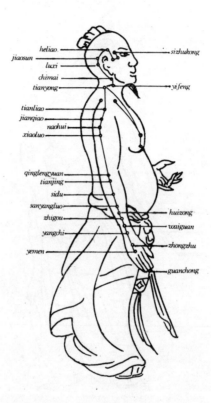

(12) The Tri-*jiao* Channel of Hand-*Shaoyang*

This channel starts at the *guanchong* point at the tip of the ring finger and runs up along the arm to meet with the *Du* channel at the *dazhui* point before going over the shoulder to the clavicle and spreading in the chest. Then, linking with the pericardium, it runs through the diaphragm to the upper-, middle- and lower-*jiao*. One of its branches appears at the *tanzhong* point and runs up along the neck to the posterior border of the ear before going round the face and ending below the eye. Another branch starts behind the ear and runs through the ear before meeting with the other branch on the face and reaching the lateral angle of the eye.

The malfunction of the tri-*jiao* channel may produce otopathy, aching of the eyes, sore throat, swelling of the cheeks, abdominal distention, watery distention or pain in the shoulder and arm.

Diagrams of *Jingluo* and Acupoint

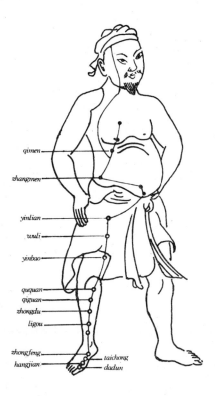

qimen
zhangmen
yinlian
wuli
yinbao
ququan
qiguan
zhongdu
ligou
zhongfeng
hangjian
taichong
dadun

(13) The Liver Channel of Foot-*Jueyin*

This channel starts at the *dadun* point at the tip of the big toe and runs along the instep and the medial side of the leg to the pubic region before going round the genitals and arriving at the lower abdomen and the liver to link with the gallbladder. Then it runs through the diaphragm and spreads in the ribs before going up along the back of the trachea to the throat and then to the eyes. Finally, it moves up along the forehead to meet with the *Du* channel at the vertex. One of its branches starts at the liver and runs up through the diaphragm before entering the lungs to link with the Lung Channel of Hand-*Taiyin*. Another branch starts at the eyes and moves down along the cheeks to the inner surface of the lips.

The malfunction of the liver channel may produce pain in the vertex of the head, dry throat, fullness sensation in the chest, hernia, vomiting or lumbago.

Diagrams of *Jingluo* and Acupoint

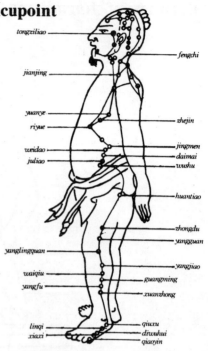

tongziliao

fengchi

jianjing

yuanye

riyue

zhejin

weidao

juliao

jingmen

daimai

wushu

huantiao

zhongdu

yangguan

yanglingquan

yangjiao

waiqiu

guangming

yangfu

xuanzhong

linqi

qiuxu

xiaxi

diwuhui

qiaoyin

(14) The Gallbladder Channel of Foot-*Shaoyang*

This channel starts at the *tongziliao* point at the lateral angle of the eye and runs up to the temple before turning down to the back of the ear and moving up again to the shoulder to meet with the *Du* channel at the *dazhui* point and reach the supraclavicular fossa. One of its branches starts at the back of the ear and goes into the ear proper before running along the front of the ear to the back of the lateral angle of the eye. Another branch starts at the lateral angle of the eye and runs down to the *daying* point and back up to a place under the eye socket, where it goes further down to the neck and the chest and through the diaphragm to link with the liver and the gallbladder. Then it goes even more down to the side of the lower abdomen and circles the pubic region before arriving at the hip region. Another branch starts at the clavicle and runs down along the armpit and the side of the chest through the *riyue*, *juliao* and *huantiao* points before going further down along the thigh and the knee to the *qiuxu* point near the ankle and arriving at the *qiaoyin* point on the tip of the toe.

The malfunction of the gallbladder channel may produce migraine, swelling and pain in the armpit, bitter taste, dizziness, and pain in the submental region or pain in the lateral side of the thigh and the knee.

EXERCISES

Clouds Setting Off Rainbow

Sit cross-legged with left hand on right shoulder and right hand on left shoulder. Turn head to the left and look ahead to the left. Inhale and exhale slowly. While exhaling, keep body relaxed and shoulders and elbows lowered. Inhale and exhale 12 times and turn head slightly to the right. Return to the starting position and repeat the whole process with "left" and "right" reversed.

This exercise can treat fullness in the chest and abdomen and resist the upward floating of *qi* in deficiency condition.

Rubbing the Gate of *Jing* with Palms

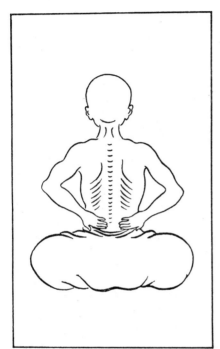

Inhale with nose and hold breath. Place palms and rub them until they get warm and then use palms to rub both sides of lower back whilst slowly exhaling with nose. The "gate of *jing*" refers to the two soft spots on lower back. Rub them 36 times before sitting quietly for a whilst at the end of the whole process.

This exercise may reinforce kidney *qi*, nourish the five *zang* organs and dispel cold and dampness.

Relaxing Feet Through Heels

Sit at ease with legs straightened. Place hands at the root of thighs with your mind focused on points of rubbing. Inhale lightly and rub forward along the medial side of legs to heels. Return to the starting position and repeat the whole process 12 times.

This exercise may treat wind-dampness-cold syndromes and pain in the leg and knee.

Soothing Chest Depression by Regulating *Qi*

Sit cross-legged with hands clenched gently. Swing right fist to the left along with left one whilst turning head to the right and left fist to the right along with right one whilst turning head to the left. Exhale gently with mouth whilst swinging fists and turning head but inhale slowly with nose whilst returning both fists to the middle part of body.

This exercise can treat fullness in the chest.

Seated on a Mat and Floating on Water

Sit cross-legged with arms slightly bent at elbow and palms facing up as if propping up the sky. Inhale slowly and direct qi down to abdomen and other body parts before exhaling slowly. Repeat the inhaling and exhaling movements nine times. Then press palms down and inhale and exhale another nine times.

This exercise may treat abdomen edema due to the *yang* deficiency.

EXERCISES

Rubbing *Dantian* and Regulating *Qi*

Sit cross-legged with right palm placed at *dantian* and left palm over right palm. Rub *dantian* in circles gently, and inhale and exhale naturally.

This exercise may treat hypofunction of the small intestines with cold manifestations.

Placing Hands at Abdomen and "Holding Up the Moon"

Sit upright with fingers of both hands interlocked at lower abdomen. Close eyes and concentrate on lower abdomen. Inhale whilst relaxing abdomen but exhale whilst drawing in abdomen.

This exercise may treat abdominal pain and stomachache.

Twisting *Tianzhu* and Getting *Qi* to Flow

   Tianzhu (neck) refers to the *qi* column linking the human body with its natural surroundings in *qigong*. Twisting *tianzhu* can activate *qi* and promote blood circulation.

   Sit cross-legged with head slightly lowered. Twisting neck to the left with shoulders turning in the same direction. Get fingers of both hands interlocked and push them down to the left side of body. Look at fingers. Return to the starting position and repeat the whole process 24 times with "left" and "right" reversed.

   This exercise can treat headache and other diseases caused by wind-cold pathogen.

Rubbing Face and Getting It Beautiful

Keep eyes closed for a moment when you wake up from a night's sleep or a noon nap. Place the back of thumbs together and rub them until they get warm. Then rub eyelids with the back of thumbs nine times. With eyes still closed, rotate eyeballs to the left nine times and right as many. Then, a moment later, open eyes and rotate eyeballs to the left nine times and right as many. This part of the exercise is effective for wind-heat syndromes and eye diseases.

Rub the back of thumbs until they get extremely warm. Then rub both sides of nose up and down 36 times when thumbs are quite warm. This part of the exercise may help nourish the lungs.

Rub spots at the outer corner of both eyes, each 36 times. Then rub spots at the inside corner of both eyes near the nose, each also 36 times. This part of the exercise may improve eyesight.

Place palms together and rub them until they get extremely warm. Rub both sides of face 90 times. This part of the exercise may get your face beautiful and delay the appearance of wrinkles.

EXERCISES

Angling by the Lake

Sit upright with legs straightened. Raise arms forward and keep them in line with legs, hands formed into hollow fists. Draw in arms and feet slowly before straightening them out. Inhale whilst drawing in arms and feet but exhale whilst straightening them out. Look straight ahead.

This exercise may treat pain in the waist and lower extremities.

The Dragon Flying and the Tiger Running

Sit cross-legged with eyes closed. Rotate tongue until you get a mouthful of saliva, or the "divine water." Gargle with it 36 times before swallowing it in three gulps. Make sounds when you swallow it and imagine that you are sending it down into *dantian* at lower abdomen. Return to the starting position and repeat the whole process three times.

This exercise may regulate and coordinate all the channels in the body.

Lao Zi Banishing the Wind

Sit cross-legged with spine upright. Clench left hand into fist and push it against upper left side of body. Open right palm naturally and put it gently on right knee. Concentrate on the affected part of body. Inhale deeply and direct *qi* towards the diseased spot. Return to the starting position and repeat the whole process with "left" and "right" reversed.

This exercise may cure paralysis, furuncle and diseases caused by wind pathogen.

Rubbing Clouds and Relaxing Sleeves

Sit upright with legs straightened. Place right foot flatly and bend left leg. Then stretch out left arm to the left, and rub abdomen with right hand, first clockwise nine times and then counterclockwise as many. Breathe naturally with your attention focused on the mind. Return to the starting position and repeat the whole process with "left" and "right" reversed.

This exercise may help treat pain in the shoulder and back and indigestion.

Water Flowing on a High Mountain

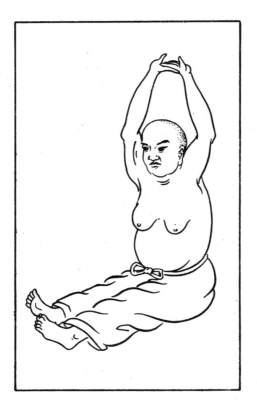

Sit upright with both legs straightened. Raise hands and keep their fingers interlocked overhead. Push hands up with the help of body as if holding a heavy stone before placing hands on top of head. Repeat this movement nine times.

This exercise will dispel *qi* stasis in the back and relax muscles.

Rubbing the Nape of Neck

Sit cross-legged with ears and head covered with hands. Inhale gently and exhale slowly with nose. Breathe 12 times before combing hair, tapping head and rubbing face.

This exercise may help alleviate incessant pain caused by the attack of wind pathogen, refresh the brain and relax the mind.

Beating the Drums and Plucking the Zither

Sit upright with right leg bent at a big angle and left leg at a small one. Rub palms until they get warm, and rub left sole with right warm palm and right sole with left warm palm until they also get warm. Then sit upright with legs crossed and hands placed on knees. Exhale with mouth nine times.

This exercise may regulate blood and *qi* vessels and treat diseases in the tri-*jiao*, dim sight and asthenia.

Sitting in Silence

Sit at ease with palms gently placed on knees. Twist body to the left and right as much as possible. Inhale when you do the twisting movement and exhale when you return to the starting position.

This exercise may regulate qi, remove blood stasis and cure miscellaneous diseases.

Flicking the Nape of Neck and Ears Echoing with Sound

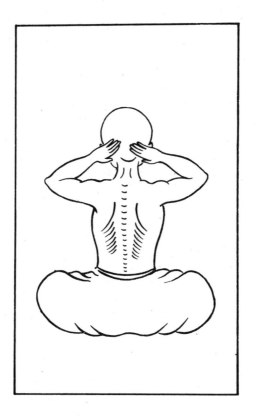

Cover *tiangu* (ears) with forefinger over middle finger of each hand on the back of head. Flick middle fingers with forefingers as if beating a drum. Repeat the flicking movement 24 times in rotation for each forefinger.

This exercise will refresh the mind and improve hearing.

Han Xiangzi* Using *Qi*

Sit at ease with legs crossed. Rub eyes with palms and place clenched hands at sides. Inhale whilst drawing in abdomen and sending *qi* up to upper body but exhale whilst relaxing abdomen and delivering *qi* down to lower body.

This exercise is effective for *qi* and blood deficiency.

* Han Xiangzi is one of the Eight Immortals in the Chinese legend.

EXERCISES

Turning the Windlass

Sit cross-legged and raise arms to sides. Rotate right arm clockwise 18 times and counterclockwise as many, as if turning a windlass. Return to the starting position and repeat the whole process with "left" and "right" reversed. Breathe naturally and keep your balance when you do the rotating movement.

Pushing Against Restraint

Sit upright with legs straightened. Bend right leg and place left foot near the root of left leg. Then put right hand on left hand with palms facing downward and raise them up to the left as much as possible. Look ahead to the right and breathe 24 times. Return to the starting position and repeat the whole process with "left" and "right" reversed.

This exercise is good for paralysis.

Fish Frolicking in the North Sea

Lie on stomach with arms and legs straightened. Raise both arms and legs up to the back before lowering them. Inhale whilst raising arms and legs but exhale whilst lowering them. Repeat the raising and lowering movements 12 times.

This exercise may help cure cholera, indigestion and stagnancy of *qi* in the chest and abdomen.

Lying on White Snow and Keeping Body Relaxed

Lie on back with body relaxed. Inhale and exhale deeply and evenly whilst rubbing chest and abdomen back and forth with hands.

This exercise is effective for indigestion and stuffiness in the chest.

Flowers Glittering in Hair

Stand upright with arms hanging at sides and feet shoulder-width a-part. Raise arms up as much as possible with palms down. Grasp ground with toes and keep anus contracted. Inhale with nose and exhale with mouth nine times.

This exercise is good for abdominal distention and pantalgia.

Liu Hai* Teasing Frog

Stand at ease with arms hanging at sides and feet together. Take a step forward with left foot and grasp ground with soles. Then clench hands and place them at waistside with knuckles facing down. Inhale with nose and exhale with mouth 12 times. Return to the starting position and repeat the whole process with "left" and "right" reversed.

This exercise is effective for tension, pain, stagnancy of *qi* and diseases caused by wind-cold pathogen.

* Liu Hai is an immortal child in the Chinese legend.

EXERCISES

Cleansing the Mind in Fresh Breeze

Stand at ease with arms hanging at sides and feet together. Take a step forward with left foot to form a T-shaped stance. Raise right arm with palm facing inward and place the back of left hand at waistside. Turn body to the left and look ahead to the left. Inhale whilst turning to the left but exhale whilst turning slightly to the right, both nine times. Keep the entire body relaxed.

This exercise is good for cardiac pain.

Adjusting the Flow of Blood and *Qi*

Stand with arms hanging at sides and feet shoulder-width apart. Bend over and hold right foot with left hand and left foot with right hand. Inhale after you turn slightly to the left and exhale after your body returns to the normal position. Repeat the breathing and turning movements with "left" and "right" reversed.

This exercise is effective for the flow of blood and *qi*.

The Black Dragon Wagging Its Tail

    Stand at ease with arms hanging at sides and feet shoulder-width apart. Bend over and press hands downward in front of legs, fingertips of hands in line with toes of feet. Exhale when you bend over but inhale when you straighten out your body. Repeat the above movements 24 times.

    This exercise is good for lumbago.

Liuzijue

Sit still and click teeth for two hours at midnight. When you have a. mouthful of saliva, swallow it in several gulps. Pronounce such sounds as "he," "xu," "hu," "sou," "chui" and "xi." In so doing, you can get rid of diseases in the five *zang* organs.

Points to remember: Lend an ear to yourself when you pronounce those sounds and prolong each of them as much as possible.

The six-character formula, or *liuzijue* in the Chinese language, is a traditional health-keeping exercise in China. Based on the *wuxing* principle and other theories, this exercise has played a great part in curing diseases and improving health and is therefore practiced widely in China. This exercise has had several versions, and some of them should be done with time and direction taken into account.

Paying Respect to Void with the Mind Still

Stand at ease with arms hanging at sides and feet shoulder-width apart. Lower head to chest and hold hands level in front of abdomen, with left hand over right one. Clear your mind of distracting thoughts. Inhale and direct *qi* down to chest and abdomen before exhaling deeply. Return to the starting position and repeat the whole process 17 times.

This exercise is good for cardiac pain.

Singing Songs and Getting *Qi* and Blood to Flow

Stand at ease with arms hanging at sides and feet shoulder-width apart. Raise left hand to the left with mind focused on the left before breathing evenly to get *qi* and blood to flow on the left side of body if there is something wrong with the circulation of *qi* and blood on the left. Repeat the whole process with "left" and "right" reversed if *qi* and blood fail to circulate on the right side.

This exercise is effective for the stagnancy of *qi* and blood.

Plucking Flowers and Getting *Qi* to Flow

Stand at ease with arms hanging at sides and feet shoulder-width apart. Raise left arm forward and rub it with right hand whilst breathing evenly. Return to the starting position and repeat the whole process with "left" and "right" reversed. This exercise is good for pain in the arm, shoulder and back.

Looking Up at Heaven and Down at Earth

Heaven is *yang* and earth is *yin*. Live in between and you can absorb *qi* from both of them and get it to flow in the five *zang* organs and limber up your muscles and joints.

Stand at ease with feet shoulder-width apart and hands clenched. Bend over slowly and push fists down as much as possible before straightening up slowly and raising fists overhead. Inhale before you bend over and hold breath when you take a bending position, and exhale when you straighten out. Return to the starting position and repeat the whole process nine times.

With muscles and joints limbered up and *qi* and blood flowing smoothly, you can cure yourself of lumbago, chest tightness, dyspnea and arthrosis.

Taking a Glance at Flowers on Horseback

Stand at ease with right foot in front and arms hanging at sides. Stretch out arms to sides with right hand in front as if propping up something. Look at right hand with body turned back slightly before returning to the starting position. Inhale whilst turning body back but exhale whilst returning to the starting position. Repeat the whole process nine times on each side.

This exercise is effective for dysentery.

Wuqinxi (1) —Tiger Form

Stand with hands clenched at sides and feet shoulder-width apart. With bated breath, lower head and push fists forward like a hungry tiger pouncing upon its prey. While keeping breath, imagine you are holding a heavy object with hands and then lifting it without much difficulty. Inhale deeply and direct *qi* down to abdomen whilst straightening up and you will feel *qi* flowing throughout body. Return to the starting position and repeat the whole process 32 times.

Wuqinxi (2) — Bear Form

Stand with hands clenched at sides and feet together. Stretch out arms to sides with right arm higher than left arm and look obliquely forward. Move one foot aside and grasp ground firmly with soles. Inhale when you direct *qi* down to abdomen but exhale when you relax waist and hips. Return to the starting position and repeat the whole process 15 times.

This form may help strengthen the lower back and alleviate abdominal distention.

Wuqinxi (3) — Deer Form

Stand with fists at sides and feet shoulder-width apart. With bated breath, lower and turn head to the back, mind concentrating on the *weilu* point at the coccyx. Then turn head back to the front before drawing in kidneys and jumping on tiptoe. Be sure to get neck moved and whole body shaken when you come down to the ground with heels. Return to the starting position and repeat the whole process 20-30 times.

EXERCISES

Wuqinxi (4) — Ape Form

Stand with arms hanging at sides and feet slightly apart. With bated breath like an ape, raise left hand up to head level as if embracing a tree and place right hand at abdomen as if holding a fruit. Lift left foot up to knee level with tiptoes pointing downward and keep right leg slightly bent. Inhale deeply and direct *qi* down to abdomen. With this position remaining unchanged, inhale and direct *qi* down to abdomen again and again until beads of sweat start running down your face. Return to the starting position and repeat the whole process with "left" and "right" reversed.

Wuqinxi (5) — **Bird Form**

Stand with arms hanging at sides and feet together. With bated breath, hold head high like a flying bird before taking a step forward with right foot and joining hands at eye level in front of face with one hand on the other. Keep your mind focusing on the body part near the *weilu* point and you will feel light enough to fly in the air. Try to strengthen your waist and the part above it.

EXERCISES

Exercises in the First Month

According to ancient practice in China, the first lunar month of the year belongs to *yin* (寅), third in the twelve earthly branches, and in addition corresponds to the Tri-*Jiao* Channel of Hand-*Shaoyang* in the *jingluo* system and *tai* in the sixty-four hexagrams. What you have to bear in mind in this month is that *qi* arises at 11 p.m. and you'd better face north in practice, and when *yang* emerges, heaven and earth and all other things are produced. In other words, it is not time to destroy but to create and not time to take away but to give.

(1) *Lichun* (the Beginning of Spring)

The time between 11 p.m. and 3 a.m. every day in this month is good for the following exercise. Sit cross-legged on bed with one hand above the other on one knee. Turn body to the left and right with neck bent forward. Return to the starting position and repeat the above movements 15 times on each side. Then, sitting upright with neck erect, click teeth and inhale and exhale with mouth before swallowing saliva in three gulps.

This exercise is good for *qi* stasis, headache and pain behind the ear and in the shoulder, back and elbow.

Exercises in the First Month

(2) *Yushui* (Rain Water)

The time between 11 p. m. and 3 a. m. every day in this month is also good for the following exercise. Sit cross-legged on bed with one hand above the other on one knee. Twist head to the left and right along with body turn. Return to the starting position and repeat the above movements 15 times on each side. Then, sitting upright and facing forward, click teeth and inhale and exhale with mouth before swallowing saliva in three gulps.

This exercise is good for stasis in the tri-*jiao* channel, deafness, sweating due to general debility, ophthalmagia and pain in the cheek.

Exercises in the Second Month

The second lunar month of the year belongs to *mao* (卯), fourth in the twelve earthly branches, and in addition corresponds to the Large Intestine Channel of Hand-*Yangming* in the *jingluo* system and *dazhuang* in the sixty-four hexagrams. What you have to bear in mind in this month is that *qi* arises at 1 a.m. and you'd better face northeast in practice. Be sure to keep yourself calm, avoid both cold and heat and nourish *shen* and *qi* in practice.

(1) *Jingzhe* (the Waking of Insects)

The time between 1 and 5 a.m. every day in this month is good for the following exercise. Sit cross-legged on bed with clenched hands obliquely above knees. Try to push elbows backward as much as possible and thrust them 30 times. Then twist neck to the left and right and click teeth 36 times before inhaling and exhaling and swallowing saliva.

This exercise is effective for pathogens in the lower back, spine, lungs and stomach as well as the yellow discoloration of the sclera, dry mouth, edema in the face, hoarseness, blurred vision and sores.

Exercises in the Second Month

(2) *Chunfen* (Spring Equinox)

The time between 1 and 5 a.m. every day in this month is also good for the following exercise. Sitting cross-legged on bed, raise hands and push them forward, and in the meantime turn head from the left to look far into the distance. Return to the starting position and repeat the above movements 42 times on each side. Then, sitting upright and facing forward, click teeth 36 times before inhaling and exhaling and swallowing saliva in nine gulps.

This exercise is good for fullness in the chest, pain in the shoulder, general debility of the *jingluo* system, toothache caused by pathogens, swollen neck, deafness, tinnitus and cutaneous pruritus.

112

Exercises in the Third Month

The third lunar month of the year belongs to *chen* (辰), fifth in the twelve earthly branches, and in addition corresponds to the Small Intestine Channel of Hand-*Shaoyang* in the *jingluo* system and *mei* in the sixty-four hexagrams. What you have to bear in mind in this month is that *qi* arises at 3 a.m. and you'd better face northeast, and with *yang* rising and *yin* receding all things develop. Be sure to go to bed and get up early every day in this month so as to nourish the visceral-*qi*, reinforce the liver and replenish the kidneys.

(1) *Qingming* (Pure Brightness)

The time between 1 and 5 a.m. every day in this month is good for the following exercise. Sitting cross-legged on bed, stretch out one arm to side and pull the other arm backward to form a bow-drawing position, with the hand in front turned into palm and the hand at the rear into fists. Return to the starting position and repeat the whole process 24 times on each side. Then click teeth, inhale and exhale deeply before swallowing saliva. This exercise is effective for pathogenic factors in the lower back, kidneys, intestines and stomach as well as deafness, stiffness in the neck, lassitude in the loin and leg and pain in the arm and elbow.

Exercises in the Third Month

(2) *Guyu* (Grain Rain)

The time between 1 and 5 a.m. every day in this month is also good for the following exercise. Sitting cross-legged on bed, raise left arm as high as possible with palm turned up and place right palm in front of the left side of chest. Keep this posture for a whilst with an even breath. Return to the starting position and repeating the whole process 35 times on each side. Then click teeth and breathe deeply before swallowing saliva. This exercise is good for blood stasis in the spleen and stomach, the yellow discoloration of the sclera, swollen cheeks, arthralgia and nosebleed.

Exercises in the Fourth Month

The fourth lunar month of the year belongs to *si* (巳), sixth in the twelve earthly branches, and in addition corresponds to the Pericardium Channel of Hand-*Jueyin* in the *jingluo* system and *qian* in the sixty-four hexagrams. *Qian* stands for vigor, strength and pure *yang*. What you have to bear in mind in this month is that *qi* arises at 5 a.m. and you'd better face east, and with the union of heaven and earth all things are produced. Be sure to go to bed and get up early so as to absorb fresh and pure *qi*.

(1) *Lixia* (the Beginning of Summer)

The time between 3 and 7 a.m. every day in this month is good for the following exercise. Sit on bed with legs bent and eyes closed. Hold breath and pull one knee with hands towards chest. Return to the starting position and repeat the pulling movement 35 times on each side. Then, sitting upright with legs crossed, click teeth and inhale and exhale before swallowing saliva.

This exercise may cure diseases caused by pathogenic wind-dampness and blockade of channels as well as dysphoria with heat sensation in the limbs and chest.

Exercises in the Fourth Month

(2) *Xiaoman* (Grain Full)

The time between 3 and 7 a.m. every day in this month is also good for the following exercise. Sit upright on bed with legs crossed and one hand raised and the other pressing against bed. Stretch out both arms and look at the hand above. Return to the starting position and repeat the whole process 15 times on each side. Then, with body remaining upright, click teeth and inhale and exhale before swallowing saliva.

This exercise will help get rid of pathogens in the internal organs, fullness and discomfort in the chest and hypochondrium, dysphoria, flushed face and the yellow discoloration of the sclera.

Exercises in the Fifth Month

The fifth lunar month of the year belongs to *wu* (午), seventh in the twelve earthly branches, and in addition corresponds to the Heart Channel of Hand-*Shaoyin* in the *jingluo* system and *gou* in the sixty-four hexagrams. *Gou* stands for the union of *yin* and *yang*, the gentle and the strong. What you have to bear in mind in this month is that with fire growing and water declining you can nourish the lungs and replenish the kidneys. Another thing you have to remember is that *qi* arises at 7 a.m. and you'd better face southeast in practice.

(1) *Mangzhong* (Grain in Ear)

The time between 3 and 7 a.m. every day in this month is good for the following exercise. Stand upright with legs slightly apart and arms hanging at sides. Lean backward and raise hands overhead before twisting body to the left and right as much as possible with eyes looking up. Repeat the twisting movement 35 times on each side. Then, sitting upright with legs crossed, breathe evenly and click teeth 36 times before inhaling and exhaling several times and swallowing saliva.

This exercise may be effective for consumption in the kidneys, pain in the heart and hypochondrium, eclampsia, amnesia, coughing, vomiting, headache and flushed face.

Exercises in the Fifth Month

(2) *Xiazhi* (Summer Solstice)

The time between 3 and 7 a. m. every day in this month is also good for the following exercise. Sit at ease with left leg bent and right leg straightened. Hold right leg with fingers of both hands interlocked and kick it forward. Return to the starting position and repeat the whole process 35 times on each side. Then, sitting upright with legs crossed, click teeth and inhale and exhale slowly before swallowing saliva.

This exercise may help cure diseases caused by wind-dampness pathogens, pain in the wrist and knee, kidneys, back and loin and heaviness in the body.

Exercises in the Sixth Month

The sixth lunar month of the year belongs to *wei* (未), eighth in the twelve earthly branches, and in addition corresponds to the Lung Channel of Hand-*Taiyin* in the *jingluo* system and *dun* in the sixty-four hexagrams. What you have to bear in mind in this month is that *qi* arises at 9 a.m. and you'd better face south. Do not regulate *yin* and *yang* in a forced way because the former is weak and the latter strong.

(1) *Xiaoshu* (Slight Heat)

The time between 1 and 5 a.m. every day in this month is good for the following exercise. Sit on left foot with hands touching bed behind the back. Extend right leg and withdraw it forcefully. Return to the starting position and repeat the straightening and withdrawing movements 15 times on each side. Then, sitting with legs crossed, click teeth and inhale and exhale before swallowing saliva.

This exercise is effective for pathogenic wind-dampness in the leg and lower back, lung distention, dry cough, hemiplegia, abdominal distention and pain, asthma, prolapse of rectum, asthenia and mental change ableness.

Exercises in the Sixth Month

(2) *Dashu* (Great Heat)

The time between 1 and 5 a. m. every day in this month is also good for the following exercise. Sit cross-legged with fists touching bed. Turn head and lift shoulders before looking backward. Return to the starting position and repeat the whole process 15 times on each side. Then click teeth and inhale and exhale before swallowing saliva.

This exercise is effective for syndromes in the neck, chest and back caused by pathogenic wind, cough, asthma, thirst, fullness in the chest, pain in the upper abdomen, shoulder and back, apoplexy, difficulty in micturition, sore skin and amnesia.

Exercises in the Seventh Month

The seventh lunar month of the year belongs to *shen* (申), ninth in the twelve earthly branches, and in addition corresponds to the Gallbladder Channel of Foot-*Shaoyang* in the *jingluo* system and *pi* in the sixty-four hexagrams. What you have to bear in mind in this month is that *pi* stands for obstruction in which *yin* and *yang* cannot unite because of obstruction in heaven and earth. Be sure to avoid rash action, keep body and mind relaxed and preserve *shen* and *qi*. Don't forget facing south in practice because *qi* arises at 11 a.m. in this month.

(1) *Liqiu* (the Beginning of Autumn)

The time between 1 and 5 a.m. every day in this month is good for the following exercise. Sit cross-legged with palms flatly on floor and body pushed up. Keep body movements coordinated so as to regulate the circulation of *qi*. Inhale whilst pushing up body but exhale whilst lowering body. Return to the starting position and repeat the whole process 36 times. Then, keeping body in an upright position, click teeth and swallow saliva.

This exercise may help restore lost *qi* and eliminate stagnant *qi* in the kidneys and cure pain in the chest and on the rib, dim complexion, headache and ophthalmagia.

Exercises in the Seventh Month

(2) *Chushu* (the Limit of Heat)

The time between 1 and 5 a. m. every day in this month is good for the following exercise. Sit upright with legs crossed and clenched hands in front of chest. Turn head and body to the left and right, 24 times on each side. Rap back 18 times when you turn head and body once. Then, with body remaining upright, click teeth and inhale and exhale before swallowing saliva.

This exercise is good for diseases caused by wind-dampness pathogens, pain in the chest, back and ribs, asthma, cough and indigestion.

Exercises in the Eighth Month

The eighth lunar month of the year belongs to *you* (酉), tenth in the twelve earthly branches, and in addition corresponds to the Stomach Channel of Foot-*Yangming* in the *jingluo* system and *guan* in the sixty-four hexagrams. What you have to bear in mind in this month is that *qi* arises at 1 a.m. and you'd better face southwest in practice. Be sure to keep yourself calm, restrain *shen* and *qi*, consolidate and nourish the original *qi* so as to provide basis for the production of elixir because the wind blows above the earth and all things grow to maturity.

(1) *Bailu* (White Dew)

The time between 1 and 5 a.m. every day in this month is good for the following exercise. Sit cross-legged with hands placed on knees. Turn head and body to the left and right whilst pushing palms downward. Return to the starting position and repeat the whole process 15 times on each side. Then, keeping body in an upright position, click teeth and inhale and exhale before swallowing saliva.

This exercise is effective for lumbago due to pathogenic wind-dampness, panic, mania, sweating due to debility, speechlessness caused by sore throat, dim complexion, sleepiness with frequent yawning and some nervous disorders.

Exercises in the Eighth Month

(2) *Qiufen* (the Autumn Equinox)

The time between 1 and 5 a. m. every day in this month is also good for the following exercise. Sit cross-legged with palms stopping ears. Swing head to the left and right, 15 times on each side. Then, keeping body in an upright position, click teeth and inhale and exhale before swallowing saliva.

This exercise is effective for pathogenic wind-dampness, edema, cold in the stomach, abdominal distention, cough and asthma.

Exercises in the Ninth Month

The ninth lunar month of the year belongs to *xu* (戌), eleventh in the twelve earthly branches, and in addition corresponds to the Bladder Channel of Foot-*Taiyang* in the *jingluo* system and *bo* in the sixty-four hexagrams. What you have to bear in mind in this month is that *qi* arises at 3 p.m. and you'd better face southwest in practice. Be sure to control nocturnal emission and astring *shen* because *yin* grows strong and *yang* weak.

(1) *Hanlu* (Cold Dew)

The time between 1 and 5 a.m. every day in this month is good for the following exercise. Sit upright with legs crossed. Raise arms to sides and palms facing each other. Then lift and lower body 15 times before turning it to the left and right, 15 times also on each side. Then, with body remaining upright, click teeth 36 times and inhale and exhale for a whilst before swallowing saliva.

This exercise helps cure pathogenic wind-dampness, headache, pain in the ribs, lacrimation, nosebleed and hemorrhoid.

Exercises in the Ninth Month

(2) *Shuangjiang* (Frost's Descent)

The time between 1 and 5 a.m. every day in this month is also good for the following exercise. Sit with legs bent and hands holding feet. Kick legs forward and withdraw them whilst keeping a grip on feet. Return to the starting position and repeat the kicking and withdrawing movements 35 times. Then, sitting upright with legs crossed, click teeth 36 times and inhale and exhale for a whilst before swallowing saliva. This exercise is effective for lumbago due to pathogenic wind-dampness, stiffness in the leg and foot, headache, muscular atrophy, hematochezia, difficulty in micturition and beriberi.

Exercises in the Tenth Month

The tenth lunar month of the year belongs to *hai* (亥), last in the twelve earthly branches, and in addition corresponds to the Liver Channel of Foot-*Jueyin* in the *jingluo* system and *kun* in the sixty-four hexagrams. *Kun* stands for submission which means that you should adapt yourself to nature. What you should bear in mind is that *qi* arises at 5 p.m. and you'd better face west in practice. Be sure to go to bed early and get up late in this month so as to warm and nourish *shen* and *qi* and ward off pathogenic factors.

(1) *Lidong* (the Beginning of Winter)

The time between 1 and 5 a.m. every day in this month is good for the following exercise. Sit cross-legged with left hand on left knee and right hand on left elbow. Turn body to the left and right and look sideways. Return to the starting position and repeat the turning movement 15 times on each side. Then push palms forward 15 times and look sideways. Click teeth and inhale and exhale before swallowing saliva.

This exercise is good for stagnancy in the chest and hypochondrium, pathogenic factors, lumbago, oppressed feeling in the chest, dysphagia, hypoacusis, edema in the face and ophthalmagia.

Exercises in the Tenth Month

(2) *Xiaoxue* (Slight Snow)

The time between 1 and 5 a. m. every day in this month is also good for the following exercise. Sit cross-legged with left hand on left knee and right hand on left elbow. Pull left hand to the left and right hand to the right. Return to the starting position and repeat the pulling movement 15 times on each side. Click teeth and inhale and exhale before swallowing saliva.

This exercise is effective for pathogenic wind-dampness, noxious heat, distention and pain in the lower abdomen, acute asthma and blood stasis.

Exercises in the Eleventh Month

The eleventh lunar month of the year belongs to zi (子), first in the twelve earthly branches, and in addition corresponds to the Kidney Channel of Foot-*Shaoyin* in the *jingluo* system and *fu* in the sixty-four hexagrams. What you have to bear in mind in this month is that qi arises 7 p. m. and you'd better face northwest in practice. Try to keep body still so that *yang* will arise.

(1) *Daxue* (Great Snow)

The time between 11 p. m. and 3 a. m. every day in this month is good for the following exercise. Stand at ease with left leg raised to chest level. Hold left foot with hands and kick it down. Return to the starting position and repeat the whole process 15 times on each side. Click teeth and swallow saliva before inhaling and exhaling.

This exercise is effective for pain in the leg and foot due to pathogenic wind-dampness, pathogens, hot mouth, dry tongue, dysphoria, cardiac pain, jaundice, spouting bleeding from anus, frequent urination, anorexia and panic.

Exercises in the Eleventh Month

(2) *Dongzhi* (the Winter Solstice)

The time between 11 p. m. and 3 a. m. every day in this month is also good for the following exercise. Sit with legs straightened. Place fists on knees and push them sideways. Return to the starting position and repeat the pushing movement 10 times on each side. In the meantime, inhale and exhale and click teeth before swallowing saliva.

This exercise is effective for pathogenic cold-dampness in the channels running through hands and feet, flaccidity with cold feet, drowsiness, pain in the shoulder, back and ribs and abdomen, fullness in the chest, constipation, swollen neck, cough, cold at the lower back and frostbite.

EXERCISES

Exercises in the Twelfth Month

The twelfth lunar month of the year belongs to *chou* (丑), second in the twelve earthly branches, and in addition corresponds to the Spleen Channel of Foot-*Taiyin* in the *jingluo* system and *lin* in the sixty-four hexagrams. What you have to bear in mind in this month is that *qi* arises at 9 p. m. and you'd better face northwest in practice, and that with heaven and earth closed *yang* goes into hiding and *yin* exerts its influence so that everything hides itself and you can avoid cold and remain warm. Be sure to stay away from pathogenic wind-cold and keep your muscles and bones unhurt.

(1) *Xiaohan* (Slight Cold)

The time between 11 p. m. and 3 a. m. every day in this month is good for the following exercise. Sit upright with legs crossed. Raise left arm and place right palm on bed, eyes looking up to the left. Return to the starting position and repeat the raising movement 15 times on each side. Then, with body remaining upright, click teeth and inhale and exhale before swallowing saliva.

This exercise is good for vomiting, abdominal distention, anorexia, dysphoria, difficult urination and defecation, dry mouth, the yellow discoloration of the sclera, listlessness and drowsiness.

Exercises in the Twelfth Month

(2) *Dahan* (Great Cold)

The time between 11 p. m. and 3 a. m. every day in this month is also good for the following exercise. Sit on left foot with palms touching bed behind back. Extend right leg as forward as possible. Return to the starting position and repeat the extending movement 15 times on each side. Then, sitting upright with legs crossed, click teeth and inhale and exhale before swallowing saliva.

This exercise is effective for stagnancy of *qi* in the channels, stiffness of body, pain at the base of tongue, granuloma in the thigh and knee, pain in the instep, abdominal distention, bowel sound and indigestion.

STYLES

Sitting Exercise

Take a sitting position in practice with body still or in *dong*. There are various forms for sitting exercise such as sitting at ease with legs crossed, sitting with the lower part of one leg on the same part of the other leg, sitting with left foot tucked under right thigh and right foot under left thigh and sitting on a bed or a chair with feet flatly on ground.

Standing Exercise

Take a standing position in practice with body still and motionless but your mind clear of distractions and breath regulated. Points to remember: Keep joints slightly bent, crotch open, head erect, body upright, shoulders relaxed and elbows lowered so that you can enter a state of *jing* (stillness). This position, seen often in health-keeping exercises and *wushu* practice, is used by various *qigong* schools as a basic method to build up *qi*.

Walking Exercise

    This exercise is usually done when you take a walk. Twist and turn head and limbs along with breath and mind concentration so that you can get *qi* and blood circulated all over body and cure yourself of diseases. It is extremely good for the strengthening of muscles and bones, the regulation of blood and circulation of *qi*.

Lying Exercise

When you do this exercise, you can lie on back, on side or on stomach with hands and legs taking various positions. This exercise has been dealt with by health-keeping masters in ancient China. The lying exercise is usually regarded as an auxiliary one and is suitable for those who are not so strong.

Taoist Exercise

There are various styles and methods in Taoist *qigong*, but all of them lay emphasis on the cultivation of *qi* and *neidan* (the combination of *jing* and *qi* through *shen*). Their characteristic features are paying much attention to the changes of *yin* and *yang* and *wuxing*, and exploring the mystery of human body. That is why the human system is fairly complete, its requirements for exercises and explanations to reactions obtained in practice are detailed. However, the most important in the exercise is the cultivation of both mind and body and the coordination of man and nature.

Buddhist Exercise

Based on "know the universe and learn about the trueness of yourself," the Buddhist exercise lays emphasis on a state in which you are tranquil and without any thoughts. In other words, you are required to sit in meditation and learn Buddhist principles so as to get rid of distracting thoughts and purify the mind. These principles can be found in Buddhist exercise such as *zhiguan* (focusing on the mind and observing things there) of the Tiantai sect, *chanding* (sitting with attention focusing on the mind) of the Chanzong sect and yoga of the Mizong sect.

Therapeutic Exercise

    Based on traditional Chinese medicine, the therapeutic exercise may help prevent and cure diseases and improve health. This exercise is often regarded as a kind of important method to cure diseases in China, and you can find explanations in such classical books as *Huang Di Nei Jing*, *Yang Xing Yan Ming Lu* and *Zhu Bing Yuan Hou Lun*.

STYLES

Confucianist Exercise

This Confucianist exercise is used to train the mind with emphasis on the cultivation of moral character. When you do this exercise, you are required to pay attention to the correctness of physical movements and concentration of the mind, nourishing *qi* and the harmony of body and mind. Moreover, sitting in meditation, cultivating moral character and nourishing *qi* are important in the Confucianist exercise and much have been written about it since ancient China.

Wushu-Qigong Exercise

The *wushu-qigong* exercise, also called internal work in *wushu*, is a kind of method to improve internal work. At first, it is used for defense in fighting against attackers and now has developed a style of way to keep fit.

The basic requirements for this exercise are the accumulation of the internal *qi* at the *dantian* region and the harmony of willpower, *qi* and strength. Lay emphasis on the training of *qi* at *dantian* in practice and you will improve your agility, invigorate your internal organs and strengthen your bones and muscles.

A number of boxing routines in *wushu* may be called *wushu-qigong* exercises, such as *taijiquan* (*taiji* boxing), *baguazhang* (eight-trigram palm) and *xingyiquan* (form-and-will boxing).

Static Exercise

The static exercise requires that you keep body motionless in practice. This exercise is used to lay groundwork for progress in *qigong* practice, helping get rid of distracting things and focus attention on the mind. That is why it is said to help you "feel the bigness of heaven and earth when you keep yourself calm."

Dynamic Exercise

This exercise requires that you, guided by the mind and spurred on by physical movements, get the internal *qi* in *dong* in a certain way so as to achieve the harmony of internal and external work, regulate the flow of *qi* and promote blood circulation. This exercise may be found in traditional *daoyin, xiangxing* (imitation) *qigong* and massage exercises.

BASIC REQUIREMENTS
FOR PRACTICE

Zheng

The term here refers to the erectness of postures and reasonableness of mental activity.

The human body is by nature gracefully and symmetrically construct-ed. But it is distorted, to varying degrees, by daily work and other physi-cal activities. Thus, the restoration of this symmetry is an important way of tapping its latent ability and improving health. That is what "going back into void" as described in *qigong* books really means. Keep physical movements correct and you can make your posture best and achieve the harmony of all body parts — the left and the right, the upper and the low-er and the inside and the outside, thus laying foundation for further prac-tice.

The reasonableness of mental activity is another requirement for you to fulfill after making your physical movements correct. When you do *qigong* exercises, keep yourself calm and without any disturbances and losses of *qi*. And be sure to make yourself free of distracting thoughts and mental burdens in daily life.

As part and parcel of various *qigong* exercises, *zheng* can be used to put internal activities in order so as to achieve the harmony of mental activi-ty and physical movements.

BASIC REQUIREMENTS

Jing

    Jing (stillness) is important in *qigong* and entering a state of *jing* (stillness) is a special method to protect your body and mind against external disturbances and avoid unnecessary losses of energy so that your cranial nerves can take a full rest and have a good mechanism for conserving energy.

    Qi should be accumulated and circulated in a state of *jing* (stillness). In addition, *jing* (stillness) can help you know more about the law of *dong* within your body and of your surroundings, and after getting rid of barriers to perception you will have a deeper understanding of the world. It is for this reason that various styles of *qigong* regard *jing* (stillness) as the only method to lay foundation for progress in *qigong* practice. As a saying goes in *qigong* books, "*Jing* (stillness) can make the internal structure of your body so compact and solid that you will be able to protect yourself against pathogenic wind."

    By laying emphasis on *jing* (stillness), we are not denying the need for *dong*. *Jing* (stillness)-induced *dong* is considered to be of a high grade, one *dong* that never ceases in the body. The coordination of *jing* (stillness) and *dong* is just the time for the balance of *yin* and *yang*.

Song

Diseases are usually caused by tension, and *song* is a method to get you relaxed and your body parts coordinated.

Song should take place in your body, including your internal organs such as the spinal column, hips, *dantian* and joints. Keep your body relaxed but not flaccid or loose. The other thing is to keep your mind relaxed, leaving it free of distracting thoughts or concentrating too much on what you are doing, especially on the reactions of your body occurring in practice. Only in this way can you get yourself relaxed to the full.

Song applies to all aspects of *qigong* practice, with your breathing even, continuous, thin and deep, movements gentle and slow and mental activity peaceful.

BASIC REQUIREMENTS

Xi

Xi or *tiaoxi* is one of the three basic points for attention in *qigong*, the other two being the regulation of physical movements and of mental activity.

There are quite a few breathing methods in *qigong*. *Zhongxi* or *taixi*, as mentioned in *Xing Ming Gui Zhi Qian Shu* (A Comprehensive Collection of Methods on the Training of *Shen* and Regulation of *Jing* and *Qi*) published in the Qing Dynasty, refers to such a breath that goes all the way to the *mingmen* point through the midline of back and links with the prenatal *qi* as a result of mutual attraction. The second method is *fushi huxi*. That means that you expand your lower abdomen whilst inhaling but contract it whilst exhaling. You can also do it quite abnormally, contracting your lower abdomen when you inhale but expanding it when you exhale. The third one is *pifu huxi* (breathing through the skin) which requires you to feel all the pores of your body are open to the outside so that you can exchange *qi* for air. The fourth is *guixi*. When you breathe in this way, you are doing it like a tortoise. The fifth is *shuxi* (counting breath), and when you do it, try to count your breath in a quiet way. The last but not the least is *tingxi* (listening to breath), during which time you can sense your breath in a quiet way.

In a word, the regulation of breath should be gentle and light and without any noise or obstruction, and when you have a vague idea of your breath, you will have achieved the harmony of *shen* and *qi*.

Kong

Kong (emptiness) means relieving the tensions of the body and mind in practice. And only in this way can you make it possible to train *shen* whilst regulating *jing* and *qi*.

Wuji produces *taiji* and then *yin* and *yang*, *bagua* and all other things in the world. *Kong* is in fact a state of supreme void and therefore plays a key role in making progress in practice. As masters in ancient China put it, the genuine *qi* arises when you feel tranquil and void in your mind. And void here takes place on the basis of human life.

Keeping in a state of void, you can gradually get rid of acquired clumsiness and distracting thoughts and return to the natural state of pureness and clarity.

BASIC REQUIREMENTS

Shun

Shun means that all the physical movements and postures and mental activity should be natural and in conformity with the law of *dong* in human life.

Specifically speaking, when you are "open" or "close" or turn body, all your movements should be continuous and unbroken with the upper and the lower, the front and the back, the inside and the outside in coordination. In addition, cling to your program for training and leave your body unforced or you will get your body hurt. As for the styles of exercise, priority should be given to those that suit your condition, emotion and character. Last but not least, keep yourself away from cold or heat in any season, attain calm and peace through the balance of *yin* and *yang*, and live a natural life for strength and harmony. With all aspects of your life natural, you will find everything smooth in *qigong* practice.

Dao

Dao or *daoyin* refers to various physical movements of the human body such as extending or contracting the limbs, bending or lifting the head, walking or lying, reading aloud or reciting a poem and breathing. This may help regulate *shen* and *qi*, nourish the body and mind in order to keep fit and prolong life. That is to say that with your bones and muscles in *dong* and attention focused on your mind, you can relieve fatigue and anxiety, dispel pathogenic factor, remove stagnancy in the channels and direct the smooth flow of *qi* in the body. In so doing, you will make your *qi* flow constantly in your body just as "running water never becomes stale and a door-hinge never gets worm-eaten."

The *daoyin* exercises are mentioned in quite a few historical records, such as "a bear climbing the tree and a bird stretching its claws" in *Zhuang Zi* (Book of Master Zhuang), 40-odd *daoyin* diagrams in *Dao Yin Tu* (*Daoyin* Exercises Illustrated) from a tomb of the Han Dynasty (206 B.C.-220 A.D.) unearthed in Changsha, Hunan Province and over 260 forms of *daoyin* exercise in *Zhu Bing Yuan Hou Lun* published in the Sui Dynasty (581-618).

BASIC REQUIREMENTS

Guan

Guan or *guanxiang* (looking and thinking) is used to regulate mental activity. It is usually divided into *fanguan* (looking inside) and *waiguan* (looking outside).

Fanguan means looking at yourself. When you do this, imagine you are looking at your internal organs and getting to know something about the function of your body. In doing so, you can learn more about yourself and keep yourself fit, feeling as if you were holding the moon and making your heart clean in a fresh breeze. *Waiguan* means watching things and phenomena in the world. In so doing, you can get your internal organs well coordinated and live in harmony with your environment. Many things can be the objects of observation, including fleeting clouds in the sky and brawling streams on the earth. This method can also be used to cure ailments. When you feel hot, you may think of ice, and when you feel cold, you can look at fire.

This method has been regarded important in traditional *qigong* exercises, and many skills of this kind have developed such as *guanchan* (looking at *chan*), *guanxin* (looking at the mind), *guanzizai* (observing nature), *guanxiang* (looking at reality) and some others.

Bao

Bao (holding) refers to the unity of physical movements and the concentration of mental activity. This term is explained as "adhering fast to simplicity" in *Dao De Jing* and as "combining the mind with the body and cultivating mental concentration so as to achieve mental stability" in *Xing Ming Gui Zhi Quan Shu*. Such positions as holding a ball in standing exercise and putting palms together in static exercise are called *xingbao* (the unity of physical movements), sending the regulated original *shen* to *dantian* is called *shenbao* (concentration of thought) and closing your ears and eyes to the outside world called *yibao* (concentration of willpower).

Bao is widely applied in *qigong* exercises, especially those containing such positions as sitting cross-legged, holding legs together, grasping the ground with toes and drawing in chin. However, a deep meaning of the term is to get *jing*, *qi* and *shen* coordinated so as to enhance the vitality of your body. That is to say you have internal and external work, movements of your upper and lower body parts, and yourself and your environment well coordinated. Only in this way will you be able to enter a state of *bao*.

Shou

This term means that when you regulate all the links of your body you should focus your attention on an object in or outside your body.

The object of *shou* may be an acupoint like *baihui*, a region like *dantian*, a body part like the lower abdomen and the site between the eyebrows or natural landscape like a mountain or a pine tree or conception or sensation. Yet the most important is *dantian*.

Shou may help you get rid of distractions and focus attention on one thought, thus making it possible for you to enter a state of *jing* (stillness) very soon. When you focus attention on some mental activity, you will get your *qi* accumulated at *dantian* and achieve almost the same results as you do through acupuncture treatment. Scientific researches in recent years show that mind concentration can really improve the self-regulation of the human body and the function of the nervous and internal systems.

Points for attention: Focus proper attention on mental activity and feel the existence of concentration on the one hand and the non-existence of it on the other.

图书在版编目（CIP）数据

气功图谱：英文/余功保著.
—北京：新世界出版社，1995. 1
ISBN 7-80005-247-8

Ⅰ. 气…

Ⅱ. 余…

Ⅲ. 气功-图谱-英文

Ⅳ. R214-64

中国气功图谱

余功保　著

*

新世界出版社出版

（北京百万庄路 24 号）

北京大学印刷厂印刷

中国国际图书贸易总公司发行

（中国北京车公庄西路 35 号）

北京邮政信箱第 399 号　邮政编码 100044

1995 年（英文）第一版

ISBN 7-80005-247-8

03000

14-E-2925S